ESTATE PLANNING THAT WORKS

How to Ensure Your Family is Provided for Long-term, Keep Your Assets Safe, and Save Thousands on Legal Fees

ANNA EIKEN

Disclaimer

This book is intended for informational and educational purposes only. It is not a substitute for professional legal advice, and no legal or financial relationship is established by reading this book. The strategies, forms, and recommendations presented are provided for your convenience and should not be relied upon as legal advice. Estate planning laws vary by jurisdiction, and individual circumstances differ. We strongly recommend consulting with a qualified attorney or financial professional before making any estate planning decisions or utilizing any of the forms provided in this book. The authors and publishers are not responsible for any actions taken based on the contents of this book.

Contents

Avoid Probate and Minimize Taxes

Consider Costs and Legal Pitfalls

Yearly Review and Maintenance

Introduction

 "A good plan is like a road map: it shows the final destination and usually the best way to get there."

H. Stanley Judd, author of "Think Rich."

Planning ahead is an essential aspect of life. Whether you are setting goals for personal development, securing your financial future, or building a successful business, a good plan provides direction and security. As the old adage goes, a failure to plan is a plan to fail. Yet, many people overlook the value of planning—often until it's too late.

In your personal life, planning might mean pursuing higher education, advancing your career, nurturing relationships, or safeguarding your health. Financially, good planning is all about budgeting, managing investments, and preparing for retirement. In business, planning involves setting growth strategies, managing risks, and ensuring long-term stability.

However, one critical but often neglected aspect of financial security is **estate planning**. Estate planning is the process of organizing your assets and making decisions about how they will be managed or distributed after your passing. It is not just for the wealthy; estate planning is for anyone who wants to protect their loved ones, minimize taxes, and live with peace of mind that your assets are secure beyond your lifetime. According to **Investopedia**, estate planning involves creating documents such as wills, trusts, and powers of attorney to ensure that your assets are handled according to your wishes.

If you're like most people, you might find the idea of estate planning to be overwhelming and delay taking action. Most people admit they are unsure about where to start, worried about the costs, and confused by all of the legal jargon. Estate planning is often seen as a daunting task, full of complex legalities and endless paperwork. This is where I come in. I understand your concerns—and I wrote this book to guide you through the process of managing your estate. It is designed to be the only resource you'll need to fully understand estate planning from start to finish.

By reading this book, you'll discover the **shortcuts** to getting your estate plan right the first time. You'll learn how to save thousands on legal fees, avoid common pitfalls, and fully protect your family and assets for the future. This isn't just about making a plan; it's about creating a lasting solution to permanently safeguard your legacy.

This book will give you the tools to achieve peace of mind, knowing that your family will be taken care of, your assets protected, and your wishes honored. Everyone eventually reaches an age where they experience nagging fears about estate planning. Instead of worrying about legal loopholes, unnecessary probate delays, and burdensome taxes, you will enjoy peace of mind knowing your planning will secure your assets. This book will give you the confidence that you've done everything to provide for your loved ones—while avoiding costly mistakes.

In this book, you'll learn the **L.E.G.A.C.Y. framework**, a comprehensive and step-by-step approach to estate planning. Here's a quick overview of what each chapter covers:

Lay the Foundation: Chapters 1 and 2 will teach you to understand the basics and get started with the right mindset.

Establish beneficiaries: Chapter 3 will show you how to make sure the right people receive your assets.

Get your documents ready: Chapters 4, 5, and 6 will guide you through the process to create your wills, trusts, and healthcare directives.

Avoid probate and minimize taxes: Chapters 7 and 8 contain everything you need to learn how to protect your assets and maximize savings.

Consider costs and legal pitfalls: Chapter 9 will enable you to avoid common traps that could cost you time and money.

Yearly review and maintenance: Chapter 10 teaches you how to keep your plan updated to reflect changes in your life and the law.

Unlike other estate planning solutions that focus only on creating a plan, the **L.E.G.A.C.Y. framework** ensures that your estate plan adapts over time, accounting for changes in your family, finances, and the law. It's a dynamic, long-term solution designed to secure your legacy for years to come.

If you're ready to take control of your future, protect your family, and ensure your assets are safe, **this book is for you.** Together, we'll navigate the complexities of estate planning and create a solid plan that truly works for you. Let's get started securing your legacy—**now.**

Lay the Foundation

ONE

Introduction to Estate Planning

 "Estate planning is an important and everlasting gift you can give your family. And setting up a smooth inheritance isn't as hard as you might think."

Suze Orman

L et's be real: estate planning is something a lot of people avoid thinking about. But it's necessary. In fact, it is paramount! If you don't have a solid plan in place, your loved ones could face legal problems, long delays, and a litany of unnecessary costs after you're gone. No one wants to leave their family in a legal mess, but that's exactly what happens when you don't take care of these things ahead of time.

A good example of the consequences a family faces when estate planning has been ignored is of the artist formerly known as Prince. Prince passed away in 2016 with no will and no estate plan in place despite having a fortune worth $300 million. His family got stuck in years of legal battles, losing millions to lawyers. After these astronomical fees, what was left of his estate was severely reduced. Prince's case shows how not having an estate plan can create chaos. Prince's example actually illustrates how everyone should plan their estate, not just those with millions in the bank account. If the family of someone like Prince can run into legal battles and unforeseen costs due to a lack of estate planning, then anyone can. And while Prince's family still had a significant amount of assets after the whole ordeal, someone with limited assets cannot afford to let their family bear such costs after they are gone.

Therefore, it is essential to understand that estate planning isn't just for the rich and famous. It's something everyone should do, regardless of your wealth or status. It ensures that your assets— whether big or small—go to the people you want without them having to jump through endless legal hoops. It also helps avoid unnecessary legal fees and taxes, making things much easier for your family.

In this book, you'll learn how to set up a simple, effective estate plan that works for you. We'll walk you through everything, from wills and trusts to the steps you need to take to avoid probate. By the end, you'll have a plan in place that protects your assets and makes things easier for your loved ones. Are you ready to secure your assets? Good! Let's get to it.

What Is Estate Planning?

Estate planning is the process of deciding how your assets will be managed and distributed after you die or if you become unable to handle them yourself. It's not just about creating a will—it includes other important documents and steps to make sure everything is handled according to your wishes, without unnecessary legal complications.

The main goal of estate planning is to make sure your property and assets are passed on to the right people while minimizing taxes and legal fees. It also allows you to plan for situations where you might not be able to make decisions for yourself, like in cases of illness or disability.

Estate planning involves setting up the following key components:

A **Will** specifies who gets your assets and names a person to manage your estate.

A **Trust** is another way to manage and distribute your assets, often helping to avoid probate– the legal process of administering an estate.

Healthcare Directives are documents that let you outline your preferences for medical care and designate someone to make healthcare decisions for you if you cannot.

Power of Attorney appoints someone to handle your finances if you're unable to do so.

By completing these steps, you make sure your estate is handled according to your instructions. It's a way to control what happens to your assets and how your personal matters are managed. Estate planning is about taking care of these details *now* so your family doesn't have to deal with confusion or complications *later*.

Why Is Estate Planning Important?

Estate planning is crucial because it ensures that your assets are handled according to your wishes and that your family is taken care of when you're no longer around. Here are some of the key reasons why it's so important:

It protects your beneficiaries. Estate planning allows you to decide who will inherit your assets, ensuring that the right people benefit. Without a plan, state laws will determine how your assets are divided, which may not align with your intentions.

It protects young children. If you have young children, estate planning lets you appoint a guardian to care for them if something happens to you. This ensures they are looked after by someone you trust.

It eliminates family messes. Clear instructions through wills or trusts help avoid disputes and confusion among family members. This reduces the chances of conflict over inheritance, which can otherwise create long-lasting family rifts.

It spares your heirs a big tax bill. Proper estate planning helps minimize the taxes that your heirs may face when inheriting your assets. Without a plan, taxes could take a significant portion of what you intended to leave behind.

It provides you with peace of mind. Knowing that your affairs are in order and your loved ones are taken care of brings unmatched peace of mind. You can rest easy knowing that your family will avoid unnecessary stress and complications.

It ensures that your family's way of life is secure. Estate planning helps maintain your family's lifestyle by ensuring that they have access to your assets quickly and without hassle, providing financial security after you're gone. It ensures a smooth transition in the event of your death or disability so that there is minimal financial disturbance for your family.

In short, estate planning is about making sure your assets are distributed as you want, protecting your family from unnecessary hardship, and giving yourself peace of mind, knowing everything is taken care of long before you are gone.

Touching on the Basics

Let's touch on the basics to get you started. Estate planning requires a few key documents to make sure everything is handled as you intend. Here's a brief overview of the essential documents, which we'll cover in more detail in later chapters:

Will: A will outlines who gets your assets and who will manage your estate after you pass away.

Trust: Trusts help manage and distribute your assets, often avoiding the probate process and allowing for more control over how and when assets are passed on to beneficiaries.

Durable Power of Attorney: This document appoints someone to handle your financial affairs if you become unable to do so. In contrast, a **Non-Durable Power of Attorney** only stays in effect while you are capable of making decisions, automatically ending if you become incapacitated.

Beneficiary Designations: Assets like life insurance policies and retirement accounts require designated beneficiaries, which should be kept up-to-date to match your estate plan.

Healthcare Power of Attorney: This gives someone the authority to make healthcare decisions for you if you're incapacitated.

Guardianship Designations: For those with minor children, this designation names who will take care of them if you're not able to.

Letter of Intent: This non-legal document provides additional instructions or information that may not be covered in your will or other legal documents.

Before we discuss each of these documents in detail, it is important to clear up some misconceptions about estate planning.

Common Estate Planning Misconceptions

Estate planning is often misunderstood, and these misconceptions can lead people to delay or avoid creating a proper plan. Let's clear up some of the most common myths about estate planning and explain why they're incorrect. Maybe you yourself are familiar with a few of these misconceptions.

"I don't have enough assets." Estate planning isn't just for people with significant wealth. No matter the size of your estate, it's important to ensure that what you own– whether it is property, savings, or personal items–go to the right people.

"I'm too young to need an estate plan." Estate planning isn't about age; it's about being prepared. Accidents and unexpected events can happen at any time, so it's wise to have a plan in place, even if you're young.

"My digital assets will automatically be passed on to my loved ones." Digital assets like social media accounts, emails, or online financial accounts don't automatically transfer to your heirs. Specific instructions for these assets must be included in your estate plan.

"I don't need a will because I'm single with no kids." Even if you're single with no children, you still have assets and belongings that need to be distributed. A will ensures your assets go to the people or causes you care about.

"Estate planning is only about what happens after I die." Estate planning also covers what happens if you're incapacitated. It includes healthcare directives, powers of attorney, and other tools to manage your affairs if you can't.

"My family will sort everything out." Without a plan, your family may face legal challenges, delays, and disputes. Estate planning provides clear instructions to avoid confusion and family conflicts.

"A will is all I need." A will is important, but it's not the only document needed for a complete estate plan. Trusts, powers of attorney, and healthcare directives are equally important to manage your affairs properly.

"Estate planning is too expensive." While there are costs involved, estate planning can save your family a lot of money in legal fees, taxes, and probate costs in the long run. It's an investment in protecting your assets and your loved ones.

"It's a one-time task." Estate planning isn't something you do once and then forget about it. Life changes—marriage, divorce, children, or new assets—require regular updates to your plan.

"If I don't make a will, the state will get my assets." This is rarely the case. If you die without a will, your assets are usually distributed to your next of kin, but it will be according to state law, not your personal wishes. Even if you think the state law is in your favor today, it might change tomorrow. Your assets don't often go to the state, but the state law could determine what happens to them.

"I don't need a lawyer to help with estate planning." While there are DIY options, estate planning can be complex. A lawyer can help you navigate state laws, minimize taxes, and ensure that your documents are legally sound.

By addressing these misconceptions, it becomes clear that estate planning is essential for anyone who wants to protect their assets and simplify matters for their loved ones.

Why Start Now?

Are you wondering why you should start planning your estate now? The truth is that estate planning is often something people put off, but starting early has clear benefits. The sooner you begin, the better you can prepare for unexpected events and make the most of your options. Here's why early estate planning is so important:

Maximize tax benefits and asset protection. Starting your estate plan early allows you to take advantage of strategies that can minimize estate taxes and protect your assets from creditors. These strategies often work best when they are put in place well in advance.

Reduce the impacts of probate. By setting up trusts and other legal structures early, you can help your family avoid or minimize the lengthy and costly probate process. This ensures that your assets are distributed more quickly and efficiently after you pass.

Maintain planning flexibility. When you start estate planning early, you have the flexibility to adjust your plan as your life changes. Whether it's marriage, having children, or acquiring new assets, an early plan is easier to adapt over time.

Plan for a change of circumstances. Life is unpredictable, and early estate planning gives you time to prepare for unexpected events like illness or accidents. Things like healthcare directives and powers of attorney ensure that your wishes continue to be respected. This chapter explained the basics of estate planning, cleared up common myths, and highlighted the importance of starting your plan early. Starting early allows you to take advantage of tax benefits, protect your assets, and adjust your plan as needed over time. The key point is that estate planning is something everyone should do sooner rather than later to avoid complications later on.

In the next chapter, we'll cover the first step in estate planning: identifying your assets, debts, and liabilities. Congratulations, you have already made it through your introduction to estate planning! Let's keep going!

TWO

Assets, Debts, and Liabilities

" *"An asset puts money in my pocket. A liability takes money out of my pocket."*

Robert Kiyosaki, the author of Rich Dad Poor Dad

W hen it comes to personal finance and estate planning, assets and liabilities are two sides of the same coin. Both play a critical role in shaping your financial situation. Understanding the difference between the two is essential for creating a solid estate plan. In this chapter, we'll discuss how to identify your assets, debts, and liabilities so your estate plan rests on complete information and reflects your true financial situation.

Calculating Your Net Worth

Here's what you should consider when calculating your net worth:

Net worth is a straightforward calculation that shows the value of what you own (your assets) minus what you owe (your liabilities). It's an important figure because it gives a clear picture of your financial health, which is essential when planning your estate.

Why does net worth matter in estate planning? Knowing your net worth is a critical first step because it helps you understand the size of your estate. This figure influences decisions on how to distribute assets, settle debts, and make sure your estate plan covers everything. Whether your net worth is high, low, or somewhere in between, knowing where you stand is key to making informed choices about your estate.

The formula to calculate your net worth is simple:

Net Worth = Assets - Liabilities

Here's how it works:

Assets: Add up everything you own that has value. This includes your home, vehicles, bank accounts, retirement savings, investments, and personal property like jewelry or art. For example, if you own a house worth $300,000, a car worth $20,000, and have $50,000 in savings, your total assets would be $370,000.

Liabilities: Add up everything you owe. This includes mortgages, loans, credit card debt, and any other outstanding debts. For example, if you have a mortgage of $200,000 and $10,000 in credit card debt, your total liabilities would be $210,000.

Simply put, once you subtract liabilities from assets, you get your net worth.

Let's take a look at what your results will look like once you have calculated your net worth.

Positive Net Worth: If your assets are greater than your liabilities, you have a **positive net worth**. This means you own more than you owe, which is generally a good position to be in.

Negative Net Worth: If your liabilities are greater than your assets, you have a **negative net worth**, meaning you owe more than you own. While this isn't ideal, knowing your situation helps you address debts and adjust your estate plan accordingly.

Understanding your net worth is a key part of estate planning as it directly impacts how you manage your assets and handle your debts. It's the foundation of your estate plan.

What Are Assets?

An asset is any resource expected to provide future economic benefit to its owner. In estate planning, assets represent everything you own that contributes to your net worth. These come in various forms, each with unique characteristics and value.

Current assets are those that can be quickly converted to cash. These include cash, checking accounts, savings accounts, accounts receivable, and short-term investments. **Fixed assets**, on the other hand, are long-term resources that you own and use to generate income or wealth. Unlike current assets, fixed assets are not meant for quick sale or conversion to cash. Examples of fixed assets include real estate, vehicles, and equipment.

Assets can also be classified as **tangible** or **intangible**. Tangible assets are physical items that hold economic value, such as property, jewelry, furniture, and collectibles. Intangible assets, while lacking a physical form, still provide economic benefits. These include patents, trademarks, copyrights, goodwill, and intellectual property.

Another way to categorize assets is based on their use. **Operating assets** are those actively used in daily operations and are crucial for generating income or value. Examples include business equipment, inventory, and real estate used for business purposes. In contrast, **non-operating assets** are not directly involved in daily operations but still hold value, such as investment properties, unused land, or excess cash reserves.

Understanding these different types of assets is essential in estate planning, as it allows you to see the full scope of what you own. Each type of asset plays a role in your overall financial situation. Knowing how your assets are classified ensures that your estate plan is thoroughly accounted for and accurate.

Identifying Your Assets

You are now ready to take the steps necessary to identify your assets. Identifying your assets is one of the most important steps you will take in planning your estate. It helps you clearly define what you own. This step is essential for determining the total value of your estate, assuring your valuable assets are protected from unnecessary taxes and legal fees, and making informed decisions about how your estate will be managed and divided. Whether you plan to leave assets to heirs or not, knowing exactly what you own and how it will be handled is crucial to getting it right.

An **asset search** is a critical part of this process. This involves creating an accurate inventory of your financial portfolio. Every asset, no matter the size, must be counted. Assets will likely appreciate in value over time, so even if an asset has a low value right now you must still count it. Conducting an asset search matters because it guarantees the **completeness of your estate inventory**, helps with **debt settlement**, ensures **fair distribution** of your assets among your beneficiaries, and supports proper **tax planning** to minimize the tax burden on your heirs.

There are different methods for conducting an asset search in estate planning. These include:

A full review of **financial statements and documents** provides information on bank accounts, investment portfolios, and retirement accounts.

Checking **real estate records** to ensure all property you own is properly accounted for.

A comprehensive list of **business interests**, including any partnerships, shares, or other business assets you may own, mitigates tax liabilities and legal issues.

Searching **public records and filings** for information on assets like real estate holdings and liens prevents complex problems later on.

Examining **tax returns** can reveal financial assets and liabilities.

Reviewing **insurance policies** identifies benefits or payouts tied to your estate.

Listing **digital assets**, such as online accounts, intellectual property, and cryptocurrencies, ensures no stones are unturned.

These are the steps you want to take to identify your assets properly.

Create a comprehensive asset inventory. Start by listing all your assets, both tangible and intangible. Don't forget to include **digital assets,** such as online accounts, intellectual property, and digital currencies.

Document ownership of your assets. Make sure you have clear documentation proving ownership of each asset. This can include deeds, titles, or any other legal documents that confirm your ownership. As part of this process, collect all necessary paperwork that supports your estate. Organizing these documents ensures that everything is in order when needed.

Review and Update Regularly. Estate planning isn't a one-time task. As you acquire new assets or sell old ones, your asset list should be updated regularly to reflect these changes.

By identifying and documenting your assets thoroughly, you create a clear picture of your estate and can ensure everything is handled according to your wishes. This step provides the foundation for a solid estate plan and helps avoid legal complications later.

Valuing Your Assets

Valuing your assets is key to getting your estate plan right. **Asset valuation** is the process of determining the value of specific properties, such as stocks, bonds, buildings, machinery, or land. This process is typically used when an asset is being sold, insured, or transferred. Asset valuation is essential in estate planning as it helps you understand the current worth of your assets, identify any factors that could impact their value in the future, ensure fair distribution, and minimize tax liabilities.

There are different ways to determine the value of your assets, depending on the type of asset and the purpose of the valuation. Here are some common methods:

Cost Method is an approach that values an asset based on the original cost of acquiring or producing it, factoring in depreciation over time. This is often used for physical assets like machinery or buildings.

The **Market Value Method** assesses the current value of an asset based on its price in the open market. For example, real estate is often valued by comparing it to similar properties recently sold in the same area.

The **Base Stock Method** involves valuing inventory based on a fixed base stock level, ensuring the valuation reflects stable prices. It's commonly used for inventory management in businesses.

The **Standard Cost Method** values an asset based on predetermined or "standard" costs rather than actual costs. It's often used in manufacturing to estimate costs for production.

These methods accurately assess the value of your assets and ensure that they are properly accounted for in your estate plan. This will help you make informed decisions about how to manage, protect, and distribute your assets effectively.

Understanding Liabilities

Understanding liabilities will help you accurately determine your net worth. **Liabilities** refer to obligations or debts owed to someone else. They are financial responsibilities that you are required to settle, whether through payment, services, or other means. In the context of estate planning, liabilities include mortgages, loans, taxes, and credit card debts. Liabilities can also refer to legal or regulatory obligations, which may arise from contracts, lawsuits, or compliance issues.

Liabilities work as obligations that reduce the value of your estate. When you pass away, these debts don't disappear; they remain to be settled, typically during the probate process. Creditors may claim a portion of your estate to settle outstanding debts, which can impact what remains for your beneficiaries. It's crucial to have a clear understanding of your liabilities when creating an estate plan to protect your assets and distribute your estate according to your intended plan.

There are three main categories of liabilities:

Current Liabilities are debts that are due within a year, such as credit card balances, utility bills, or short-term loans.

Non-current liabilities are long-term debts that are not due within the next year, such as mortgages, student loans, or long-term business loans.

Contingent Liabilities are potential liabilities that may occur depending on the outcome of a future event, such as a lawsuit or guarantee on a loan.

Understanding the distinction between these liabilities is important for determining how they will be managed and settled in your estate plan. A comprehensive estate plan should therefore ensure that debts are settled without significantly diminishing the value of your assets for your beneficiaries.

Debts are a form of liabilities. Debts are financial obligations incurred during your lifetime, and they don't automatically vanish upon death. Creditors can file claims against your estate during probate to recover what they are owed. This is why including your debts in your estate plan is extremely important. By listing your debts, you protect your assets from unforeseen creditor claims, reduce the burden on your beneficiaries, and ensure a smoother probate process.

Here are the steps you should take for listing your debts.

When creating a list of debts for your estate plan, it's important to be thorough. Your list should include:

Personal Property Debts, which include all financing related to vehicles, real estate, or other personal property.

Personal Debts including credit cards, medical bills, and personal loans.

Business Debts are all debts related to businesses you own, including loans or accounts payable.

Taxes encompass all income tax, property tax, or other tax obligations.

Any other obligations, such as unpaid legal fees or debts related to legal settlements, are classified as **Other Debts**.

By documenting all liabilities and debts clearly, you ensure that your estate plan is comprehensive. To make this process even easier, I've written simple worksheets you can fill out to start your estate plan off right.

A **Net Worth Worksheet** helps you calculate your overall financial standing by subtracting your liabilities (debts) from your assets. Below is a guide on how to calculate your net worth.

Instructions for Filling Out the Net Worth Worksheet

List your assets. Use the asset inventory worksheet you've completed above to list all assets, including real estate, financial accounts, and personal property.

List your liabilities. Include any outstanding debts, such as mortgages, loans, credit card debt, and taxes.

Subtract your liabilities from your assets to calculate your net worth. This number gives you a snapshot of your overall financial health.

In the **Appendices**, you will find a downloadable **Net Worth Worksheet**. This worksheet is designed to help you organize and document your financial situation. You can fill it out to get a clear picture of your assets and liabilities, which will be a valuable tool in your estate planning process.

In this chapter, we explored the importance of understanding your assets, liabilities, and net worth in estate planning. Calculating your net worth is a key step in assessing your financial situation and preparing an effective estate plan. By accurately identifying and valuing your assets and debts, you can make informed decisions to protect your estate and ensure it is distributed according to your wishes.

The key takeaway is that understanding your financial landscape —through assets, liabilities, and net worth—gives you control over your estate and helps you plan more effectively. Now is the time to take action: use the provided worksheets to calculate your own net worth and get a clear picture of your financial standing. Congratulations! You have already begun planning your estate!

In the next chapter, we will discuss the important process of choosing beneficiaries, which will help you ensure your assets go to the right people.

Establish Beneficiaries

THREE

Choosing Your Beneficiaries

 "Our greatest responsibility is to be good ancestors."

Jonas Salk

C hoosing beneficiaries is one of the most important steps in estate planning. It's about making thoughtful decisions regarding who will inherit your assets and ensuring that the legacy you leave behind positively impacts your loved ones and future generations. By carefully selecting your beneficiaries, you help protect your family's financial well-being and make sure your wishes are honored after your passing. This chapter will guide you through the factors you need to consider when selecting beneficiaries.

What Are Beneficiaries?

A beneficiary is an individual or organization you name to receive your assets after you pass away. Beneficiary designations allow you to specify who will inherit particular assets, often bypassing the need for probate court involvement. This streamlines the process and ensures that your property is distributed as you intend.

So how does this work? Beneficiaries can be any person or organization you choose, and you can set specific conditions for how they receive their inheritance. For example, you may require that a beneficiary reach a certain age or meet other conditions, such as being married, before they can take control of the inherited property. This allows you to have control over how and when your assets are transferred.

Naming beneficiaries is crucial because it allows you to control what happens to your money and property after your death. By clearly designating beneficiaries, you reduce the potential for disputes or confusion among family members, simplifying the settlement of your estate.

In financial accounts, such as insurance policies or retirement funds, beneficiary designations take precedence over any instructions in a will. This means that changes to a will do not affect these designations, which ensures that your beneficiaries receive what you intended without delay. Additionally, unlike wills, which become part of the public record during probate, the names of beneficiaries for financial accounts remain private, offering your heirs more privacy.

Identifying Beneficiaries

There are two main types of beneficiaries:

The **Primary Beneficiary** is the person or organization who will receive your assets first. If the primary beneficiary is alive or able to take possession of the property when you pass away, they inherit your assets directly.

The **Contingent Beneficiary** is next in line to inherit your assets if the primary beneficiary cannot or does not want to take the inheritance. For example, if your primary beneficiary passes away before you do or is unable to inherit, the contingent beneficiary would receive the assets.

The key difference between a primary and contingent beneficiary is that the contingent only receives assets if the primary beneficiary is either unable or unwilling to do so. Nominating two different people for these roles ensures that even if the primary beneficiary doesn't work out, the contingent beneficiary can handle your assets according to your wishes, thereby avoiding confusion and legal mess.

Different types of beneficiaries offer various benefits and considerations, depending on your goals.

Naming your **spouse** as a beneficiary provides financial security for them and often offers tax advantages, such as deferring estate taxes. However, you should consider whether your spouse will need immediate access to liquid assets or have the ability to manage more complex investments.

For **non-spousal beneficiaries**, such as adult children, other relatives, or close friends, the benefits include ensuring that specific loved ones are taken care of. However, these beneficiaries might face higher taxes on inherited retirement accounts, which can reduce the value of the assets they receive. Careful consideration should be given to how your assets will be divided and the potential tax burdens.

Designating a **trust** as a beneficiary can give you greater control over how and when your assets are distributed. This is particularly useful for younger beneficiaries or for situations where you have specific conditions about the inheritance. Trusts can also help avoid probate, but they involve legal costs and may require ongoing management.

If you have **charitable giving goals**, naming a charity as a beneficiary allows you to leave a lasting legacy while also offering tax benefits for your estate. It's essential to clearly specify the charity to avoid any confusion or legal issues.

If you prefer to leave your assets to **multiple beneficiaries**, this allows for flexibility and the opportunity to benefit more than one individual or organization. However, it requires careful planning to ensure fairness and clarity in how assets are allocated, reducing the risk of disputes among your beneficiaries.

There are some important things to consider before choosing a beneficiary. Here are some of the key factors to keep in mind.

What are your estate planning objectives? First, consider what you want to achieve. Whether it's providing financial security for family members or supporting a charity, your *goals* should drive your decisions.

Do you have minor children? If you have minor children, you will need to set up a trust to manage their inheritance until they reach an appropriate age. Additionally, you'll need to designate a guardian to manage the trust.

Do you have a beneficiary with special needs? If this is the case, a special needs trust is essential to ensure that their eligibility for government benefits remains intact.

Do you have charitable giving goals? If you wish to include charitable donations as part of your estate plan, you must carefully consider how much of your estate to allocate to charitable causes and what tax consequences that could have.

What are your family dynamics and how might they be impacted? Consider the relationships between your beneficiaries. Leaving someone out or favoring one beneficiary over another could cause disputes. Understanding your family dynamics can help you make decisions that avoid future conflicts.

The process of selecting beneficiaries requires thoughtful consideration and planning. Here's how you can approach it:

Define your beneficiaries. Identify the individuals or organizations you want to benefit from your estate. These could include family members, friends, charities, or a combination.

Consider your relationships. Evaluate your relationships with potential beneficiaries, considering their financial needs and your personal connections with them.

Be specific in your wording. Clearly outline who will receive specific assets or percentages of your estate to avoid any confusion or disputes. The more detailed you are, the smoother the process will be for your beneficiaries.

Address tax implications.: Some assets, such as retirement accounts, may carry tax consequences for your beneficiaries. Be mindful of these and consult a professional to minimize tax burdens.

Review and regularly update your designated heirs. Life circumstances change over time. It's essential to review and update your beneficiary designations regularly to ensure they align with your current wishes.

Keep documentation updated. Ensure that your will, trusts, and any other relevant legal documents are up-to-date and consistent with your current beneficiary designations.

By considering your personal goals and the needs of your beneficiaries, you can make informed decisions that ensure your assets are distributed according to your wishes while minimizing complications for your loved ones.

When it comes to identifying **contingent beneficiaries**, there are some important considerations to make.

Contingent beneficiaries are individuals or organizations that inherit your assets if the primary beneficiary is either unable or unwilling to do so. Naming contingent beneficiaries ensures that your assets are still distributed according to your wishes, even if the primary beneficiary passes away before you do or cannot accept the inheritance for any reason whatsoever. This is an important backup in estate planning as it provides clarity and avoids litigation and the court's involvement. When a primary beneficiary is no longer able to receive the inheritance, two common Latin terms come into play: **Per Capita** and **Per Stirpes**. These terms describe how assets are distributed among contingent beneficiaries.

Per Capita means "by the head." In this distribution method, assets are divided equally among all living descendants or beneficiaries at the same generational level. Each living person receives an equal share. If a beneficiary has passed away, their share is not passed down to their descendants but is instead equally divided among the remaining living beneficiaries.

Here are some examples of contingent beneficiaries.

Let's say you have three children, and you name them as your primary beneficiaries. If one of your children passes away before you do, and you specified **Per Capita** distribution, the two remaining children would divide the assets equally between themselves. The deceased child's descendants (grandchildren) would not inherit their parent's share.

Per Stirpes means "by the branch." In this method, if a primary beneficiary passes away, their share is passed down to their descendants. This ensures that each branch of the family still receives their portion of the inheritance, even if the primary beneficiary is no longer alive.

Using the same scenario of three children, if you specified **Per Stirpes** distribution and one of the children passed away before you do, that child's share would go to their descendants (your grandchildren), rather than being redistributed to your remaining children. Each branch of the family retains their portion of the inheritance.

It's important to note that **Per Capita** and **Per Stirpes** distributions only come into play when a primary beneficiary has passed away. If the primary beneficiary is still alive, they will receive the assets as planned, and these terms are irrelevant. However, naming contingent beneficiaries and specifying how you want your assets distributed ensures your estate plan remains clear and minimizes potential legal disputes, regardless of what happens in the future.

Beneficiary Designation Form

A **beneficiary designation form** is a legal document that outlines your wishes for how specific assets or funds should be distributed after your death. It ensures that financial institutions and legal entities know who should receive the proceeds from your accounts, such as retirement plans, insurance policies, or other financial products. Each of these accounts typically has its own separate beneficiary designation form. Unlike a will, which may cover a broader range of assets, beneficiary designations bypass probate, allowing the specified assets to be distributed directly to the named beneficiaries.

There is no **one-size-fits-all** beneficiary designation form for estate planning. Different forms apply to different assets, such as life insurance, retirement accounts, and investment portfolios. Each type of asset requires its own specific form, so it's important to fill out the appropriate form for each financial product or account.

Here are some tips to remember when you fill out your beneficiary designation forms.

Remember to name all beneficiaries. Make sure you clearly name your beneficiaries to avoid any confusion. Without a named beneficiary, your assets may go through probate, which can be time-consuming and expensive.

Be sure to name both primary and contingent beneficiaries. Always list both primary and contingent beneficiaries. If the primary beneficiary is unable to receive the assets, the contingent beneficiary ensures your assets are still distributed according to your wishes.

Update for all life events. Major life events such as marriage, divorce, the birth of a child, or the death of a beneficiary should prompt you to update your beneficiary designation forms to reflect your current situation.

Carefully read the form's instructions. Each form comes with specific instructions. It's crucial to read and follow these instructions to avoid any issues or delays in asset distribution.

Think twice before naming individual beneficiaries for particular assets. For example, if you name specific individuals for certain assets, it could create unintended inequality among beneficiaries. Consider whether you want to leave equal portions or particular items to certain people.

Use caution when naming a trust as a beneficiary. Naming a trust as a beneficiary can be beneficial in certain situations, but it requires careful planning. Some assets, like retirement accounts, may have complex tax implications when left to a trust.

Use disclaimers when necessary, but be careful. A disclaimer allows a beneficiary to refuse an inheritance, passing it to the next eligible person. This can be useful in certain tax or financial situations, but it should be done carefully to avoid complications.

Keep all original forms secure. Once your forms are filled out, keep them in a secure location and ensure that your executor or loved ones know where to find them.

In the **Appendices**, you will find a downloadable **Beneficiary Designation Form.** You can use this form to clearly outline your beneficiaries for various accounts and assets. Please note that there is no universal form for beneficiary designations, so each form should be tailored to your specific circumstances.

Instructions for Filling Out the Beneficiary Designation Form

Account Holder Information: Start by filling out your personal information at the top of the form. Include your full name, Social Security Number, date of birth, current address, phone number, and email ID. This ensures that the account is properly identified and linked to you.

Account Information: Specify the type of account for which you are designating beneficiaries. This could be a life insurance policy, retirement account (such as a 401(k) or IRA), investment account, or another financial product. Include the account number to ensure clarity.

Primary Beneficiary(ies): In this section, list the individual(s) or organization(s) whom you want to receive the assets, from this account, after your death. Include their full name, relationship to you (e.g., spouse, child, friend), date of birth, and Social Security Number (if applicable). Allocate a percentage of the total assets to each beneficiary. The total percentage must add up to 100%. For example, in case of two beneficiaries, you could assign 50% to each.

Contingent Beneficiary(ies): If your primary beneficiaries are unable to receive the assets, contingent beneficiaries are next in line. Follow the same procedure as above, listing the full name, relationship, date of birth, Social Security Number, and percentage allocation. Again, the total percentage for contingent beneficiaries must equal 100%.

Signature and Authorization: Once the form is completed, review all of the information to ensure its accuracy. Sign and date the form to confirm your choices. Some institutions may require a witness or notary to validate your signature, so check if that's required.

Submitting the Form: Once the form is signed, submit it to the relevant financial institution or plan administrator. Keep a copy for your records in a secure location, and make sure your beneficiaries are aware of your plans.

In this chapter, we covered the importance of identifying and designating beneficiaries in your estate plan. Beneficiaries are essential in ensuring that your assets are distributed according to your wishes without unnecessary delays or legal complications. The key takeaway is that choosing your beneficiaries carefully is crucial. Your choices determine who will inherit your assets and how those assets will be managed. Regularly reviewing and updating beneficiary designation forms is equally important, as life events such as marriage, divorce, or the birth of children can affect your estate plan. Keeping your forms up-to-date ensures your wishes are honored throughout your lifetime.

In the next chapter, we'll explore **wills,** another critical tool in estate planning. You are doing a fantastic job learning how to plan your estate!

Get Your Documents Ready

FOUR

It's More Than Just Writing Wills

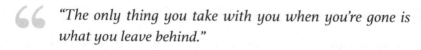 *"The only thing you take with you when you're gone is what you leave behind."*

John Allston

A will allows you to leave behind a legacy and ensure that your wishes are carried out after you pass away. While many people think of a will as simply a document that states who gets what, it is much more than that. It's a powerful tool that allows you to make important decisions about your assets, your loved ones, and how you want your legacy to be preserved. This chapter explores the significance of a will and why it is a critical part of any comprehensive estate plan.

What Is a Will?

A **will** is a legal document that outlines how you want your assets and personal property to be distributed after your death. It allows you to appoint guardians for minor children, specify how your estate should be managed, and designate who will carry out your final wishes. The primary purpose of a will is to ensure that your estate is handled according to your instructions, rather than being distributed based on state laws.

A will takes effect only after your death, allowing you to control your assets and make decisions about them throughout your lifetime. You can modify or update your will as circumstances change, ensuring that it always reflects your most recent wishes.

Here are some of the important benefits of having a will.

You retain control over your assets. A will ensures that your assets remain under your control during your lifetime. You decide who inherits your property, money, and personal items, and you can make changes whenever necessary.

You can be flexible. Life circumstances change, and so can your will. You can modify your will to address new situations, such as marriage, divorce, the birth of children, or the death of a beneficiary.

You get to include specific instructions. You can direct your gift or inheritance to serve a particular purpose, such as funding a charitable cause or ensuring a loved one's future. This allows you to customize your legacy and make sure your wishes are honored.

Don't forget the estate tax benefits. Under current tax law, there is no upper limit on the estate tax deduction for charitable bequests. This means that if you choose to leave part of your estate to a charity, it can help reduce estate taxes for your heirs.

There are some legal terms you should know when making a will.

The person who creates and signs the will is known as the **testator.** The testator outlines how their assets should be distributed and appoints individuals to manage the estate.

The person named in the will to carry out the instructions and wishes of the testator is the **executor.** The executor is responsible for managing the estate, settling debts, and distributing assets to beneficiaries.

As we covered in the previous chapter, the **beneficiaries** are the individuals or organizations designated to receive the assets and property outlined in the will. Beneficiaries can include family members, friends, charities, or other entities.

The legal process through which a will is validated by a court and the executor is given authority to distribute the assets is called **probate.** Probate ensures that the will is properly executed and that all legal and financial matters are settled before the assets are distributed to the beneficiaries.

Having a will provides peace of mind, knowing that your wishes will be carried out and that your loved ones will be taken care of according to your instructions. It's a crucial element of estate planning that offers flexibility and control over your legacy.

Types of Wills

There are several types of wills, each serving different purposes depending on your specific needs and circumstances. Here's a breakdown of the most common types of wills, their uses, benefits, limitations, and key considerations.

A **simple will** is the most straightforward type of will. It outlines who will inherit your assets, appoints an executor, and can include instructions for the care of minor children. A simple will is intended for individuals with uncomplicated estates who want to specify how their assets will be distributed and who will manage their affairs after death. There are benefits to writing a simple will. They are easy to create, provide clear instructions, and ensure that basic estate planning needs are met. One of the limitations is that simple wills *do not* account for more complex situations, such as trusts for minor children or strategic tax planning. Remember that a simple will may require updates as life circumstances change (e.g., marriage, divorce, or new children).

A **testamentary trust will** creates a trust within your will to manage the distribution of your assets after death, often for minor children or individuals who cannot manage their inheritance on their own. These types of wills are intended for parents or individuals who want to set conditions on how and when beneficiaries receive their inheritance. Some benefits of testamentary trust wills are the provision of greater control over how assets are distributed, particularly for minors or beneficiaries with special needs. They also protect assets until beneficiaries are ready to manage them. One limitation is that they require ongoing management which may lead to additional costs, such as trustee fees. Because testamentary trust wills are more complex, you may want to consider hiring an attorney to set it up properly.

A **joint will** is a single will shared by two people, usually a married couple, that outlines how their assets will be distributed upon the death of both individuals. Joint wills are best suited for couples who want to ensure their assets are distributed in the same way. They are simpler to create and can be a good option for couples. However, once a spouse passes away, the terms of the joint will cannot be changed. This can impose restrictions if circumstances change. Many legal experts advise against joint wills due to this lack of flexibility for the surviving spouse.

A **living will** is not related to the distribution of assets; instead, it outlines your wishes for medical care if you become incapacitated and cannot make decisions for yourself. Living wills are specifically for individuals who want to specify their medical preferences in case they cannot communicate or make decisions due to injury or illness. They ensure that your medical treatment preferences are known and respected while relieving family members from having to make difficult decisions on your behalf. It is important to know that living wills only cover medical decisions; all other assets will need further planning. It is a document that is part of your overall estate plan and should be paired with other important documents such as **healthcare power of attorney** to comprehensively cover your medical care.

A **nuncupative will** is an oral will made in the presence of witnesses, typically in emergency situations where the individual cannot create a written will. They are typically only used in critical or life-threatening situations when someone is unable to draft a formally written will. While they might provide a last-minute option for those who do not have one in place, many jurisdictions *do not* recognize nuncupative wills. Even in places where they are deemed valid, there are several limitations involving distributing larger assets beyond personal property. For example, real estate may not be covered by a nuncupative will. It is best to create a formally written will rather than rely on last resorts in case of emergencies.

Each type of will has its unique benefits and limitations. A **simple will** covers basic needs, while a **testamentary trust will** offers more control over how assets are distributed. A **joint will** can simplify estate planning for couples but lacks flexibility. A **living will** ensures your medical wishes are followed, but doesn't cover asset distribution. Finally, a **nuncupative will** is a last-minute solution in emergencies but should not replace a formal, written will.

When deciding which type of will is best for you, consider the complexity of your estate, your family's needs, and any specific instructions or conditions you want to include. It's also important to consult an attorney, especially for more complex wills, to ensure your wishes are clearly documented and legally binding.

Elements of a Valid Will

Let's explore the elements of a will that ensure its validity when the time comes to put it to work.

For a will to be legally valid, several important criteria must be met to ensure that it accurately reflects the testator's wishes and holds up in court. The testator must be of sound mind, meaning they have the mental capacity to understand the nature and consequences of their decisions. The testator must also be at least 18 years old to create a legally valid will. They must understand what a will is, the extent of their assets, and the people who will be affected by the distribution of their estate. The will must be signed voluntarily by the testator, without any undue influence or coercion–the decision to create and sign the will must be made freely.

In addition to these requirements, the following elements are typically found in a valid will:

Testator's Information: This includes the testator's full legal name, marital status, and details about children, if applicable. This section confirms the identity of the testator and ensures clarity about their family situation.

Asset Distribution: The will must include a section that outlines how the testator's assets will be distributed among the beneficiaries. This should be clear and specific to avoid any confusion or disputes later.

Guardian for Minor Children: If the testator has minor children, the will should name a guardian to take care of the children in the event of the testator's death.

Executor and Successor Executor: The will should name an executor (also known as a personal representative) to carry out the testator's wishes and manage the estate. It's also common to name a successor executor in case the primary executor cannot fulfill the role.

General Provisions: These are any additional clauses or provisions required by state law, such as funeral instructions or details about how debts should be handled.

Signatures: The will must be signed by the testator in the presence of at least two witnesses, who must also sign and date the will. The witnesses confirm that the testator was of sound mind and signed the will voluntarily.

Common Will Provisions

A **will provision** is a specific instruction or request made by the testator (the person creating the will) in their last will and testament. These provisions provide detailed guidance on how the testator's estate and other important matters should be handled after their death. Some provisions are legally required, while others reflect the testator's personal wishes regarding issues such as funeral arrangements, organ donation, or care for minor children and pets. By including clear provisions in the will, the testator ensures their wishes are carried out according to their intentions.

Let's cover some of the common will provisions and their purposes.

A **residuary clause** specifies how the remainder of the estate—the assets not specifically mentioned elsewhere in the will—should be distributed after all specific bequests have been made. This provision is essential to ensure that any overlooked or unexpected assets are passed to beneficiaries. It prevents any remaining estate assets from being subject to intestacy laws (where state law determines the distribution).

An **attestation clause** certifies that the will has been signed by the testator in the presence of witnesses, and that the witnesses observed the testator signing voluntarily. It's an important legal provision that helps confirm the validity of the will. The provision of proof helps avoid challenges to the will's authenticity in court.

Guardianship Designations are a provision which names a **guardian** for any minor children, should the testator pass away before the children reach adulthood. It is one of the most important provisions for parents, as it ensures the children will be cared for by someone the testator trusts, avoiding a court appointed guardian.

A **disinheritance clause** specifies individuals who are intentionally excluded from receiving any inheritance. This provision makes it clear that certain people are not to benefit from the estate, protecting intended heirs from legal disputes or challenges from those seeking to claim a share.

There is a provision which outlines the testator's preferences for **funeral and burial arrangements**, such as whether they prefer burial or cremation, specific religious or cultural practices, and the location of their final resting place. This provision provides clear guidance on the testator's wishes for their funeral and burial, helping family members make decisions during a difficult time. This often reduces uncertainty or conflicts for your loved ones after your passing.

The **Executor Appointment** provision names the individual responsible for managing the estate, carrying out the testator's instructions and overseeing the distribution of assets to beneficiaries. This ensures that a trusted person is in charge of handling the estate, fulfilling the testator's wishes. It also names a successor executor in case the original executor is unable to serve.

Beneficiary Designations identify the **beneficiaries** who will receive specific assets, such as property, bank accounts, or personal belongings. It clearly outlines how the estate will be divided among these individuals or organizations. They provide clarity on who will inherit the testator's assets.

A **conditional clause** specifies that a gift or bequest will only be made if certain conditions are met. For example, a testator might leave a sum of money to a grandchild on the condition that they graduate from college. This creates an allowance for specific conditions that must be fulfilled before the inheritance is granted. A conditional clause can also help encourage certain behaviors or ensure that beneficiaries are prepared to manage their inheritance.

By including these provisions in a will, the testator ensures that their estate is distributed properly, their loved ones are cared for, and any personal preferences are respected after their passing. Each provision plays a critical role in making the will as comprehensive and effective as possible.

State-Specific Requirements for a Will

Each U.S. state has its own specific requirements for creating a valid will. While many states share similar standards, there are important differences to be aware of depending on where you live. Below is a general overview of state-specific requirements for creating a valid will, with similar states grouped together.

In general, most states require the following for a will to be valid:

The testator must be at least 18 years old.

The testator must be of sound mind when creating the will, meaning they understand the nature and consequences of their decisions.

The will must be in writing. Verbal (nuncupative) wills are typically only allowed under special circumstances, such as imminent death.

The testator must sign the will voluntarily.

The will must be signed in the presence of at least two witnesses who are *not* beneficiaries under the will. The witnesses must also sign the document.

Most states–including **California, Texas, New York, Florida, Illinois**, and **Georgia**–follow these basic requirements for a valid will. The variations among these states primarily involve additional formalities, such as whether the will must be notarized (in some states, notarization is optional but can make the will "self-proving," meaning it can go through probate without requiring witness testimony).

Some states have special considerations you should know about.

Louisiana follows civil law (as opposed to common law in other states), meaning that wills must adhere to stricter guidelines. For example, Louisiana allows two types of wills: **holographic** (hand-written) and **notarial** (typed, signed, and notarized). Holographic wills must be entirely written, signed, and dated in the testator's handwriting.

In some states, handwritten or **holographic wills** are allowed without witnesses. States that permit holographic wills include **California, Texas, Virginia, North Carolina**, and **Pennsylvania**. However, the will must be entirely written, signed, and dated by the testator, and must clearly indicate the testator's intent to distribute their property upon death. While holographic wills may be valid in these states, they are often subject to greater scrutiny in probate court and are more likely to be contested.

A few states allow **nuncupative (oral) wills**, but only under very limited circumstances. States that permit nuncupative wills include **New York** (where they are allowed for military personnel and mariners at sea) and **North Carolina** (where they are allowed for individuals in imminent danger of death.)

Nuncupative wills are generally only valid for distributing personal property (not real estate) and require witnesses. They are typically seen as a last resort and are not recommended as a primary estate planning tool.

In many states, a will can be made **self-proving** if it is notarized. This means that the witnesses sign an affidavit before a notary, stating that they observed the testator sign the will. A self-proving will speeds up the probate process because the court does not need to contact the witnesses for testimony. States that allow self-proving wills include **Florida, California, Texas, Ohio,** and **Nevada.**

Most states require at least two witnesses to be present when the testator signs the will. However, there are differences in how witnesses are handled. **Vermont** requires three witnesses. **Louisiana** requires two witnesses, but they must sign the will in the presence of a notary public. **Ohio, Connecticut**, and **Maryland** may call witnesses to testify in probate if the will is not self-proving.

While notarization is not required for a will to be valid in most states, some states (**Florida, Nevada**, and **Ohio**) encourage it for the will to be self-proving.

It's important to check the specific requirements of your state and consider consulting with an estate planning attorney to ensure that your will meets all legal criteria.

For your convenience, a comprehensive table of **State-Specific Will Requirements** is available in the **Appendices.** You can download it to review each state's requirements, ensuring that your will complies with state laws where you reside. This table includes details like age requirements, witness counts, and allowances for holographic and nuncupative wills.

Writing a Will

Now that you know about the different types of wills, let's get into the details of writing a will. Your will is the legal document which will empower your choices after your passing. Writing a will is an important step in ensuring that your assets are distributed according to your wishes after your death. Whether you have a simple estate or more complex assets, having a clear and legally valid will provides peace of mind for both you and your loved ones. Here are the key steps to writing your will:

First, you must decide how you will write your will.

There are several ways you can create a will, depending on your personal needs and the complexity of your estate:

Use an online will maker. Online platforms offer easy-to-use tools for creating a basic will, especially if your estate is straight-forward.

Hire an estate planning lawyer. For more complex estates, hiring an attorney ensures that your will complies with state laws and reflects your detailed wishes.

Purchase a will kit or template. You can use the forms provided in this book as templates, which you can customize for your specific situation. These are ideal if you want more control over your estate planning without needing to hire a lawyer.

Write your own. If you have a simple estate and are familiar with the requirements, you can write your own will. Just ensure it meets your state's legal standards.

A clear title is a vital starting point to negate any potential challenges from the start. Begin by clearly titling your document as your **Last Will and Testament,** and include the full date of writing or signing. This makes it clear that this is your final legal will and overrides any previous versions, even if earlier versions had the same title. The date helps ensure that this most recent version takes precedence, providing an accurate marker in case of disputes.

Listing your assets is an important step. Make a detailed list of all your significant assets, such as real estate, bank accounts, investments, vehicles, and personal possessions. This list will ensure that no assets are left out of your estate plan.

You must decide who should receive your assets. Refer back to **Chapter 3** for guidance on choosing your beneficiaries. Be specific about who will receive which assets and whether there are any conditions or limitations tied to the bequests.

Once you have selected your beneficiaries, you must make another choice. Select an **executor** to carry out your wishes as outlined in your will. The executor will be responsible for managing your estate, paying off debts, and distributing assets to your beneficiaries. Make sure to choose someone trustworthy and capable of handling these responsibilities.

If you have minor children, it's crucial to appoint a **guardian** who will care for them if you pass away before they reach adulthood. This decision ensures your children will be raised by someone you trust.

You may want to leave a gift to charity after your passing. If you want to support a charity after your death, you can include a **charitable gift** in your will. This can be a specific amount or a percentage of your estate, depending on your wishes.

Make sure your will is legally signed. To make your will valid according to law, you need to sign it in the presence of at least two witnesses (depending on your state). The witnesses must also sign the document to confirm that you were of sound mind and not under duress when creating the will.

Once your will is signed, store it in a safe, secure location, such as a fireproof safe or with your attorney. Make sure it's easily accessible when needed. Tell your executor and loved ones where to find your will.

It's important to review and update your will regularly, especially after major life events such as marriage, divorce, the birth of children, or the acquisition of new assets. Keeping your will up-to-date ensures it reflects your current wishes.

By following these steps, you can create a legally valid will that reflects your wishes and provides clarity for your loved ones after your passing. Many people find the idea of writing a will to be intimidating or overwhelming. Now that you have the steps outlined and are familiar with the legal terms that apply, you likely feel a lot more comfortable with it. Writing your will is actually an empowering task that grants you and your loved ones long-term security.

In the **Appendices**, you will also find a **Will Toolkit** with downloadable forms and instructions that can guide you through creating your own will. This toolkit includes the following documents:

- Domestic Partnership with Children Will
- Domestic Partnership without Children Will
- Married with Children Will
- Married without Children Will
- Self-Proving Affidavits
- Single with Children Will
- Single without Children Will

These forms are designed to help you tailor your will to your specific needs and circumstances, making the process easier and more straightforward. Feel free to download and use them as you work through your estate planning.

There are some instructions you would want to follow when filling out your will.

Declaration: Write your full name and current address in the declaration section. This states that this is your legal will and revokes any previous wills.

Appointment of Executor: Name the person you trust to manage your estate and carry out your wishes (your executor). If your chosen executor cannot serve, name a backup (successor executor).

Distribution of Assets: List your significant assets and specify who should inherit them. Be as specific as possible to avoid confusion later. Then, include a residuary clause to explain who should receive any assets not specifically mentioned.

Guardianship for Minor Children: If you have minor children, name a guardian to care for them in case you pass away before they turn 18.

Funeral and Burial Wishes: If you have preferences for your funeral or burial, write them here to guide your loved ones.

Signatures and Witnesses: Sign your will in front of at least two witnesses (depending on your state's requirements). The witnesses should also sign and date the document to confirm that they saw you sign it and that you were of sound mind.

In this chapter, we covered the key steps to writing a will, from deciding how to create it, choosing your beneficiaries and executors, to signing it in front of witnesses to make it legally valid. The key takeaway is the importance of creating a will and regularly updating it as life circumstances change. Having a current, legally valid will ensures that your estate is managed as you intended.

We encourage you to practice writing your own will using the template provided in the **Appendices**. This exercise will help you feel more prepared and confident about the process.

In the next chapter, we will explore **trusts**, another important tool in estate planning. You are well on your way to completing your estate plan!

FIVE

Start Setting Up Trusts

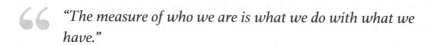 *"The measure of who we are is what we do with what we have."*

Vince Lombardi

This quote highlights the importance of taking responsibility for what you have and using it wisely. When it comes to estate planning, setting up trusts allows you to take control of your assets, secure them, and make sure that they are managed according to your wishes for future generations. Trusts provide a flexible and powerful way to protect your estate, reduce tax burdens, and provide for loved ones or charitable causes after you are gone. You might be wondering what exactly is a trust?

What is a Trust?

A **living trust** is a legal arrangement created by an individual (the grantor) during their lifetime to manage and protect their assets. In a living trust, the grantor places assets under the control of a trustee, who is responsible for managing those assets according to the grantor's instructions, both during their lifetime and after their death. Upon the grantor's death, the trust directs how these assets should be distributed to beneficiaries, allowing for a smoother transition of assets without going through probate.

A living trust functions by transferring ownership of the grantor's assets to the trust. The grantor can serve as the trustee and maintain control of the assets while alive, or they may appoint another person or institution to act as the trustee. Upon the grantor's death, the trustee (or successor trustee, if the grantor was the initial trustee) manages the assets according to the terms outlined in the trust document, thereby ensuring distribution to beneficiaries as specified. Unlike a will, a living trust doesn't go through probate, making the distribution of assets faster and often more private.

The primary purpose of a living trust is to protect assets and ensure their smooth transition to beneficiaries after death. It helps avoid probate and saves time and legal costs. A living trust provides privacy, as trust details do not become public records like wills. Further, a living trust protects the grantor's assets from creditors and other legal claims while ensuring the continued management of assets if the grantor becomes incapacitated.

There are some advantages to setting up a trust.

As we have just discussed, assets in a trust are distributed without going through probate court, making the process quicker and less costly. Living trusts also maintain privacy. Unlike a will, which becomes public record, the details of a trust remain private. Another advantage is incapacity protection. If the grantor becomes incapacitated, the successor trustee can step in to manage the assets without court intervention. Further, they offer flexibility. Trusts can be altered or revoked by the grantor during their lifetime, allowing changes as circumstances evolve.

Having said that, setting up a trust may also present some disadvantages. Setting up a trust typically involves higher upfront costs than creating a simple will. Trusts may also be more complex and therefore more complicated set up and maintain, especially if the grantor holds multiple types of assets. Be aware that trusts require ongoing maintenance. The grantor must ensure that all intended assets are properly transferred into the trust, which requires regular updates.

A **living trust** and a **will** serve different purposes in estate planning. A living trust allows for the transfer of assets without probate, manages assets during the grantor's lifetime (including periods of incapacity), and provides privacy. A **will** is a legal document that specifies who will inherit your assets after you die and can also name guardians for minor children. However, a will must go through probate and become a public record.

Both documents are important for comprehensive estate planning, but a living trust provides additional benefits in terms of asset management during your lifetime and avoiding probate.

While a **trust** is the legal relationship that establishes how assets will be managed and distributed, involving the grantor, trustee, and beneficiaries, a **trust fund** on the other hand refers to the legal entity that actually holds the assets placed in the trust. In simple terms, a trust sets up the rules and framework, while the trust fund contains the specific assets.

Types of Trusts

Trusts are versatile tools in estate planning, serving different purposes based on the structure and the specific needs of the grantor. Below are descriptions of common types of trusts along with examples to illustrate how each one works in practice.

It is important to understand the difference between revocable and irrevocable trusts. A **revocable trust** can be changed or canceled by the grantor during their lifetime. For instance, if you set up a trust to manage your assets but later decide to remove a beneficiary or add new assets, you can make those changes. However, when the grantor dies, the trust becomes irrevocable, meaning no further changes can be made. At that point, the assets within the trust are distributed to the beneficiaries according to the instructions laid out in the trust document—without the need for probate—which can help expedite the process.

Consider the following example. Sarah creates a revocable trust to manage her property and investments. She remains in control of the trust. And, if her circumstances change, such as having another child, she can modify the trust to include that child as a beneficiary.

An **irrevocable trust** cannot be altered once it is established. The assets in an irrevocable trust are no longer part of the grantor's estate, providing stronger protection from taxes and creditors. Here is an example of an irrevocable trust. John places his vacation home in an irrevocable trust to protect it from potential creditors and reduce estate taxes. Since he no longer owns the home, it is shielded from legal claims and will pass to his heirs tax-free.

Another type of trust is an AB Trust. An **AB trust** is used by married couples to reduce estate taxes by splitting the estate into two trusts when the first spouse passes away. One trust (Trust A) holds the surviving spouse's assets, and the other (Trust B) holds the decedent's assets, allowing both to use their estate tax exemptions. One example of an AB trust is the case of Lisa and Mike. When Lisa passes away, her estate is divided between Trust A and Trust B. Her husband, Mike, has access to Trust A for his needs, but Trust B, which holds Lisa's portion, is not subject to estate taxes. When Mike dies, their children will inherit both trusts without paying additional taxes.

You may want to consider an asset protection trust if you work in a high risk field. An **asset protection trust** is designed to shield assets from creditors or legal judgments. It is often used by individuals with high-risk professions or potential liabilities. Take David as an example of this type of trust. David, a physician, sets up an offshore asset protection trust to protect his savings from potential lawsuits related to his medical practice. While offshore trusts can be legal and useful, they must comply with all applicable tax laws and regulations to avoid any issues with legality or suspicion. Proper guidance from a qualified attorney ensures the trust is set up correctly.

A **blind trust** is one where the grantor or beneficiaries have no control over or knowledge of the specific assets in the trust. This is commonly used by public officials to avoid conflicts of interest. For example, Emily is a government official. To avoid conflicts of interest while holding public office, she transfers her investments into a blind trust. The trustee manages her assets without informing her of the specific holdings or of the decisions made.

A **bypass trust** is used to reduce estate taxes by allowing a portion of the decedent's assets to bypass the surviving spouse's taxable estate while still providing income to the surviving spouse. Consider the following hypothetical circumstance. When Robert dies, his estate creates a bypass trust for his wife, Jane. Jane can receive income from the trust, but the assets in the trust are excluded from her estate, making sure that their children will inherit them tax-free when she passes away.

A **charitable trust** is created to benefit a charity, either during the grantor's lifetime or after their death. This type of trust can provide tax deductions for the grantor. Here is one instance in which a charitable trust is optimal. George sets up a charitable remainder trust, naming a cancer research foundation as the beneficiary. The trust pays him an income during his lifetime–and, when he dies, the remaining assets go to the foundation. He also benefits from a significant tax deduction for his charitable contribution.

A **generation-skipping trust** passes assets to grandchildren, bypassing the children's generation to avoid estate taxes. You might be like the following grandmother who chose this option. Julia sets up a generation-skipping trust for her grandchildren. Instead of leaving her estate to her children, who are financially well-off, she skips a generation, making sure that her grandchildren will inherit the assets directly, avoiding estate taxes at the children's level.

A **Grantor Retained Annuity Trust, or GRAT,** allows the grantor to transfer assets into a trust while receiving annuity payments for a set period. After the annuity payments end, the remaining assets are transferred to the beneficiaries tax-free. Consider the example of Mark. Mark transfers $1 million worth of stock into a GRAT and receives annual annuity payments for 10 years. At the end of the term, the remaining assets, which have appreciated in value, pass to his children without any estate tax.

A **special needs trust** is established to provide for a disabled beneficiary without affecting their eligibility for government benefits such as Medicaid or Supplemental Security Income (SSI). For example, Jennifer sets up a special needs trust for her son, who has a disability. The trust provides for his care and expenses without disqualifying him from receiving SSI and Medicaid.

A **spendthrift trust** protects the assets from being squandered by a beneficiary who may not be financially responsible. The trustee has control over how and when the assets are distributed. You might find yourself in a similar circumstance as this mother who chose to write this type of trust. Margaret creates a spendthrift trust for her son, who struggles with managing money. The trustee ensures that the assets are distributed in smaller amounts over time to prevent him from spending the entire inheritance irresponsibly.

These examples illustrate how each type of trust serves a unique purpose, helping individuals and families achieve specific estate planning goals, from protecting assets to reducing taxes and ensuring long-term care for beneficiaries. Understanding the differences between these trusts can help you choose the right type of trust for your financial situation.

Trust Distributions

Now that you have a solid understanding of the different types of trusts, it is important to know about the types of **trust distributions.**

When it comes to distributing trust assets to beneficiaries, there are different methods trustees can use based on the terms set by the grantor (the person who established the trust). These distribution methods allow flexibility in how and when beneficiaries receive the assets, helping to meet the grantor's goals and protect the financial well-being of the beneficiaries. Here are the three most common distribution methods:

First, an **outright distribution** occurs when the trustee distributes the entire amount of the trust's assets to the beneficiaries in one lump sum or at once. The beneficiaries gain full control of the assets immediately, with no restrictions or conditions attached. This method is typically used when the grantor trusts the beneficiaries to manage the assets responsibly or when the assets are not significant enough to warrant ongoing management.

As an illustration, let's say Jane establishes a trust for her daughter. Upon Jane's death, the trust's assets—$200,000 in cash—are distributed outright to her daughter, who gains immediate control over the entire sum. There are some advantages to outright distributions. They are simple, fast, and offer beneficiaries immediate access to the assets. However, be aware that beneficiaries may spend the inheritance quickly or irresponsibly, leaving them without long-term financial support.

Second, in a **staggered distribution**, the trustee releases portions of the trust's assets to the beneficiaries at predetermined intervals or ages. This method spreads the distribution over a period of time, ensuring that the beneficiaries do not receive the full amount all at once. Staggered distributions are often used when the grantor wants to ensure that beneficiaries have access to funds at different stages of life, while at the same time preventing them from spending the full inheritance too quickly.

For example, consider the following case. Robert creates a trust for his son, with instructions that one-third of the assets be distributed when his son turns 25, another third when he turns 35, and the final third when he turns 45. In this scenario, the staggered distribution presents an advantage. It provides the beneficiaries with financial support at different stages of life, reducing the risk of mismanaging the inheritance. One disadvantage to staggered distribution is that beneficiaries may experience frustration if they need more money earlier but are restricted by the trust's terms.

And third, a **discretionary distribution** gives the trustee full discretion to decide how and when to distribute the trust's assets. The trustee considers the beneficiaries' needs, requests, or circumstances and then determines the amount and timing of each distribution. This method is often used to provide financial protection to beneficiaries who may not be able to manage their money effectively due to age, incapacity, or other factors. It allows the trustee to make decisions based on the beneficiary's best interests.

Consider the case of Sarah. Sarah creates a discretionary trust for her daughter, who struggles with financial management. The trustee has the discretion to distribute money for her daughter's education, healthcare, and living expenses, but only when it's deemed necessary. In this scenario, the discretionary distribution offers maximum flexibility for managing and distributing assets according to the beneficiaries' needs. However, the beneficiaries may feel dependent on the trustee's decisions and may not receive the assets when they want or even need them.

In summary, **outright distributions** provide beneficiaries with immediate access to their full inheritance. While this offers simplicity and speed, there's the risk that beneficiaries may spend the assets quickly without long-term planning. **Staggered distributions**, on the other hand, spread the inheritance over time, giving beneficiaries access to portions of the trust's assets at specified intervals or ages. This approach offers more financial stability at key life stages, ensuring the assets are not mismanaged early on. Lastly, **discretionary distributions** allow the trustee to determine when and how much of the assets are distributed based on the beneficiary's needs. This method provides the highest level of control, ensuring that beneficiaries only receive funds when necessary, but it can create a sense of dependency on the trustee's decisions. Choosing the appropriate distribution method depends on the grantor's goals and the specific needs of the beneficiaries.

Standard Trust Clauses

Precision is an imperative part of estate planning, which brings us to **standard trust clauses.** Trust clauses define how a trust operates, outlining the roles of the trustee, beneficiaries, and the management of assets. These clauses protect the grantor's intentions and provide flexibility for the trust to adapt over time.

For instance, a **Spendthrift Clause** is often included to protect beneficiaries from poor financial decisions. Imagine Jane, a grantor, has concerns about her son Mark, who has a history of financial instability. By including a spendthrift clause in her trust, Jane ensures that Mark's inheritance cannot be sold, transferred, or claimed by creditors. This guarantees that Mark will receive financial support while protecting the assets from his poor financial decisions.

A **Discretionary Distribution Clause** gives the trustee control over when and how much to distribute. Let's say Jane's trust appoints a trustee to determine when Mark can receive distributions, based on his financial needs. This allows the trustee to distribute smaller amounts for essential needs rather than a lump sum, ensuring long-term financial stability.

In contrast, **Dynasty Trust Provisions** allow the trust to benefit multiple generations. Jane might want to ensure her grandchildren and great-grandchildren are provided for, so she includes dynasty trust provisions. The trust will continue to hold and grow the assets for future generations, avoiding estate taxes with each passing generation.

If circumstances change, **Decanting Provisions** can offer flexibility. Suppose tax laws change, or Mark's financial situation improves, the trustee can use the decanting clause to move the assets from the original trust to a new trust with updated terms to reflect those changes, without going to court.

A **Trust Protector Mechanism** appoints a third party, the **trust protector**, to oversee the trust. In Jane's case, if her trustee mismanages the assets, the trust protector can step in, replace the trustee, and ensure the proper administration of the trust.

The **Powers of Trustee Clause** is essential in defining the trustee's authority. In Jane's trust, her trustee has the power to invest in real estate, sell stocks, or manage the trust's business interests. This allows the trustee the flexibility to grow and manage the trust's assets effectively.

A **No-Contest Clause** can prevent disputes. Suppose Jane fears that her daughter, Sarah, might challenge the trust's terms. The no-contest clause states that if Sarah disputes the trust and loses, she forfeits her inheritance. This discourages any legal disputes among family members.

For any assets not specifically assigned, the **Residuary Clause** directs their distribution. In Jane's trust, any remaining assets, not explicitly mentioned in the trust document, are left to her grandchildren, ensuring that no part of her estate is left unmanaged.

Lastly, a **Minors Clause** makes sure that if Jane's grandchildren are minors when they inherit, the trustee will manage their assets until they reach a specified age—say, 25 years old. This clause ensures that the inheritance is protected and not misused by a beneficiary too young to manage it.

For example, Jane's revocable trust includes an **Amendment and Revocation Clause**, giving her the flexibility to change the trust terms as her life circumstances evolve. If Jane's family situation or financial status changes, she can modify or revoke the trust at any time during her life.

In case Jane becomes incapacitated, an **Incapacity Clause** ensures that her appointed trustee can manage her assets without needing court approval. This gives her peace of mind, knowing that her finances are in trusted hands.

A **Successor Trustee Clause** names Jane's sister, Emily, as the successor trustee if Jane is no longer able to manage the trust herself. This ensures continuity and smooth management of the trust without interruptions.

Finally, the **Distribution Upon Death Clause** specifies how Jane's assets will be distributed after her passing. Jane has outlined that her estate should be divided equally among her children, with certain assets reserved for her grandchildren's education. This clause ensures that Jane's wishes are honored after her death, much like a will.

These clauses, along with the illustrative example of Jane's trust, demonstrate how standard provisions work together to ensure the proper management, protection, and distribution of a trust's assets while adapting to changing circumstances. Life changes in ways we cannot predict, but setting up a trust is one way to guarantee your assets are protected with room to adapt.

Trust Funding

Setting up a trust fund is a critical part of ensuring that your assets are managed and distributed according to your wishes. Below are the key steps involved in setting up a trust fund, along with common mistakes to avoid during the process.

There are some steps you need to take when setting up a **trust fund.** Let's get into them. First, you must set goals for your trust. Before establishing a trust, it's important to determine your goals. Do you want to protect assets for future generations, minimize estate taxes, or provide for a specific beneficiary? Clearly defining your goals will help you make key decisions, such as the type of trust to set up and how assets will be distributed. Next, you need to choose the type of trust you want to establish based on your goals. Remember, a revocable trust offers flexibility as you can modify or revoke the trust during your lifetime. An irrevocable trust provides greater asset protection and tax benefits, but cannot be changed once it's created.

Then, you must determine the terms of the trust. These include choosing a trustee, determining distributions, and setting provisions. When choosing a trustee, you want to select someone who is reliable to manage the trust and ensure that the assets are distributed according to your wishes. This person can be a family member, friend, or professional trustee. Determine distributions by specifying when and how the beneficiaries will receive distributions–whether in a lump sum, or staggered over time, or discretionary based on their needs. In setting provisions it is important to define any specific conditions that need to be met before the assets are distributed. Typically, this means that the beneficiary has reached a certain age or achieved a milestone such as completing their education.

Once these steps are complete, you will create your trust documents.

Work with an attorney or a reliable legal service to draft the trust documents. The trust deed should outline all the terms, provisions, and instructions for managing the trust.

In the **Appendices**, you will find a comprehensive **Trust Toolkit** with downloadable forms and instructions to assist you in setting up your trust. This toolkit includes the following documents:

- Assignment of Property to Trust
- Pet Trust
- Reversal of Assignment of Property to Trust

- Revocable Living Trust for Individual with A-B Trust
- Revocable Living Trust for Individual
- Revocable Living Trust for Married Couple
- Revocation of Trust

Feel free to use these forms to make the process easier and guarantee that all aspects of your trust are properly handled. However, it is strongly recommended that these documents be reviewed by a qualified attorney to avoid potential legal issues and ensure compliance with state laws.

Finally, you will fund the trust. After creating the trust documents, you must **fund** the trust by transferring assets into it. This may include real estate, bank accounts, investments, or personal property. Ensure that ownership of these assets is transferred to the trust to make it effective.

There are some common mistakes to avoid when setting up a trust fund.

- Avoid choosing the wrong trustee. The trustee has significant responsibilities in managing the trust's assets and carrying out the distributions correctly. Selecting an unreliable or inexperienced trustee can lead to mismanagement. It's essential to choose someone who is trustworthy, financially savvy, and understands the responsibilities of the role.
- Make certain that you do not release the funds too soon. Distributing assets too early—such as to a beneficiary who may not be mature enough to handle a large sum of money—can lead to financial instability or mismanagement of the funds. Setting up staggered

distributions or allowing the trustee to use discretion can
help prevent this issue.

- You want to be thorough without adding provisions that
  are too restrictive. While provisions in a trust are
  important, being too restrictive can limit the trustee's
  ability to manage the assets effectively. For example, tying
  distributions to specific conditions that are hard to meet
  (e.g., only receiving funds after graduating from a specific
  university) can create unnecessary difficulties for the
  beneficiaries.

- Make sure that you review the trust regularly. A trust
  should be regularly reviewed to account for changes in
  laws, financial situations, or family circumstances. Failure
  to update the trust can result in outdated provisions that
  no longer reflect the grantor's wishes or the beneficiaries'
  needs.

By following these steps and avoiding common mistakes, you can
set up a trust that protects your assets and guarantees that they are
distributed according to your goals.

In this chapter, we explored the essential steps to setting up a trust
fund, including determining your goals, choosing the right type of
trust, establishing the terms, and funding it with your assets.
Trusts not only help minimize taxes but also safeguard your assets
from mismanagement and legal challenges.

It's highly recommended to seek professional legal advice when
creating a trust, as the process can be complex and mistakes can
lead to unintended consequences. Consulting with a lawyer
allows you to set up your trust correctly, in a way that aligns with
your goals.

In the next chapter, we'll discuss **Power of Attorney** and **Advance Directives**, two concepts that are equally crucial in managing your affairs effectively if you become unable to make decisions yourself. You are halfway to fully setting up your estate plan!

SIX

Powers of Attorney and Advance Directives

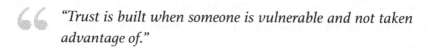 *"Trust is built when someone is vulnerable and not taken advantage of."*

Bob Vanourek

This quote highlights the essence of estate planning, especially when it comes to decisions about who will manage your affairs if you become incapacitated. When creating a plan for the future, you must trust the individuals you designate to handle your personal, medical, and financial matters. Powers of attorney and advance directives are critical tools as your disposal that allow you the opportunity to place your trust in someone reliable, someone who will respect your wishes when you're unable to communicate them yourself. These legal instruments empower trusted individuals to act on your behalf to keep your interests protected.

Understanding Powers of Attorney

Let's dive into the details of what it means to appoint someone to act on your behalf. It is critical that you understand powers of attorney when drafting this component of your estate plan. A **Power of Attorney (POA)** is a legal document that grants an individual (the "agent" or "attorney-in-fact") the authority to make decisions on behalf of another person (the "principal"). These decisions can be related to financial matters, healthcare, or other personal affairs, depending on the type of POA established. The principal chooses a trusted person to act in their best interests, especially when they are unable to make decisions themselves.

A POA gives the agent the legal authority to act on behalf of the principal. The scope of authority granted depends on the type of POA. For example, a healthcare POA allows the agent to make medical decisions, while a financial POA gives authority over financial matters like managing bank accounts or paying bills. A POA can be temporary (limited to a specific task or timeframe) or long-term (remaining in effect if the principal becomes incapacitated).

In estate planning, a POA plays a crucial role in ensuring that the principal's affairs are managed smoothly and without interruptions. Key roles include decision making authority, incapacity planning, continuity management, and healthcare decisions. The agent makes decisions based on the authority granted by the POA, whether it's related to finances, healthcare, or legal matters. If the principal becomes incapacitated, the POA ensures someone can step in to manage their affairs without needing court approval. With a POA, the agent can continue to manage financial and legal matters seamlessly, even if the principal is unable to. A healthcare POA allows the agent to make medical decisions on the principal's behalf, honoring their healthcare preferences.

Types of Power of Attorney

There are four types of power of attorney (POA) to take into consideration for your estate plan. Should you need to use a POA, knowing what each one does will help you navigate your choice and select one that best suits your needs.

One, a **healthcare POA** gives the agent the authority to make medical decisions on the principal's behalf when they are unable to do so themselves. This includes decisions about treatments, surgeries, and long-term care.

Two, a **general POA** grants broad authority to the agent to manage financial and legal matters for the principal. This authority ends if the principal becomes incapacitated.

Three, a **limited POA** is used for specific tasks or for a certain period. For example, it may allow an agent to sign documents or sell property on the principal's behalf for a particular transaction.

Four, a **durable POA** remains in effect even if the principal becomes mentally incapacitated. This makes it a vital tool in estate planning, enabling the continuity of decision-making even if the principal is unable to manage their own affairs.

A **durable POA** is often the preferred option in estate planning because it remains effective in situations where the principal is incapacitated, which is often when they need the most help. Unlike a general POA, which ends if the principal becomes incapacitated, a durable POA entitles the agent to continue managing the principal's affairs long-term, without needing a court-appointed guardian or conservator. By having a durable POA in place, the principal avoids the need for court intervention, saving time, money, and stress for their family. In setting up a durable POA, the principal can rest assured that their affairs will be handled according to their wishes, even in the event of incapacity.

Creating a Power of Attorney

By creating a power of attorney, you are preparing the opportunity for someone you trust to act in your best interests if you are unable to communicate or make decisions due to injury or illness. You are empowering yourself to retain control of your wishes against the odds of unexpected circumstances.

Setting up a Power of Attorney (POA) ensures that someone you trust can make important decisions on your behalf if you are unable to do so. Here are eight steps to creating a POA.

First, **determine which type of POA** suits your needs. Options include healthcare, financial, general, or durable POAs. We have just gone over the purposes of each one.

Second, you must choose your **agent.** Selecting the right agent is critical. The agent must be at least 18 years old (this age may vary depending on your state). They cannot be your healthcare provider. The agent should be someone you trust to act in your best interests and capable of making tough decisions. They must be willing to honor your wishes, even if others disagree. Ideally, the agent lives nearby as they may need to be available for extended periods to manage your affairs.

Third, you must decide how much authority to give your agent. You can give your agent broad authority over your affairs or limit their power to specific decisions, such as handling medical decisions or managing a particular account.

Fourth, you will need to obtain a Power of Attorney form. You'll need a legally valid form to create your POA. Each state may have its own specific form, so use the correct one! In the **Appendices**, you will find an **Incapacity Planning Toolkit** that includes downloadable forms and instructions for creating a **Durable Power of Attorney**.

Fifth, you must complete the form, sign it, and have it witnessed. Fill out the POA form with your chosen agent's details and the scope of their authority. Make sure the document is signed and witnessed according to the legal requirements in your state. This often involves signing in front of a notary or a set number of witnesses.

Sixth, give a copy of your POA form to your agent and other interested parties. Your agent must have a copy of the signed document. You may also want to provide copies to your healthcare providers, financial institutions, or any other relevant parties.

Seventh, keep your POA forms in a safe place. Store the original POA in a secure location, like a fireproof safe. Make sure that your agent and other key individuals know where to find it.

Eighth, update your POA as your circumstances change. Life circumstances change, and so may your needs. Regularly review your POA to ensure that it still reflects your wishes and that your chosen agent is still the best person for the role.

By following these steps, you can create a valid POA that provides security and peace of mind for the future.

Advance Directives

Now that you have a solid grasp on Powers of Attorney, let's get into the subject of **advance directives**. Advance directives are legal documents that communicate an individual's healthcare preferences in the event they are unable to make decisions for themselves. These directives ensure that healthcare providers and loved ones understand and honor the individual's wishes regarding medical treatment, even if the individual is incapacitated. The two main types of advance directives are **living wills** and **healthcare (medical) power of attorney** (also known as **healthcare proxy** in some states).

A **healthcare proxy** is a legal document in which you appoint someone to make healthcare decisions on your behalf if you are unable to do so. This term is sometimes used interchangeably with **healthcare (medical) power of attorney (MPOA)**. The healthcare proxy document gives authority to the appointed individual (the "proxy" or "agent") to make medical decisions based on your preferences and values.

There are different types of **advance directives** to consider. A **living will** is a written document that outlines specific medical treatments a person does or does not want if they are unable to make decisions due to incapacity. This document covers various medical interventions, allowing individuals to specify their preferences in advance. Some common decisions covered by a living will include:

- **Cardiopulmonary Resuscitation (CPR):** Individuals can state whether they wish to receive CPR if their heart stops or if they prefer a "Do Not Resuscitate" (DNR) order.

- **Ventilators:** This refers to mechanical assistance for breathing. A living will can specify whether the individual wants to be placed on a ventilator and, if so, under what circumstances.
- **Pacemakers and Implantable Cardioverter-Defibrillators (ICDs):** These devices help regulate heart function. A living will can address whether the individual wishes to have these devices used if their heart stops functioning normally.
- **Artificial Nutrition and Hydration:** This refers to feeding tubes and IV fluids. Individuals can decide whether they want artificial means of nutrition or hydration in situations where they are unable to eat or drink on their own.

A living will provides clarity to healthcare providers and loved ones about the types of life-sustaining treatment the person is willing to receive, reducing confusion during critical situations.

The purpose of each directive achieves different goals. A **living will** is designed to address specific medical situations and outline the treatments a person wishes to accept or refuse in those circumstances. A **medical power of attorney** designates someone to make healthcare decisions if the principal is incapacitated but doesn't necessarily address every possible medical situation. The agent or proxy can make decisions based on the principal's wishes or best interests in a broader range of scenarios.

Often, living wills and medical power of attorney forms (health-care proxy forms) are combined into a single advance directive document to ensure that both the specific medical preferences and the appointment of a trusted agent are in place. This provides a comprehensive approach to handling medical decisions when the individual cannot communicate their wishes.

There are some key differences between medical power of attorney (MPOA) and Durable Power of Attorney (DPOA). Mainly, these include scope of authority and duration. An MPOA, or healthcare proxy, is limited to making healthcare decisions. The MPOA agent is responsible for making medical decisions if the principal becomes incapacitated but does not have authority over financial or legal matters. A DPOA grants broad authority to an agent to manage the principal's financial and legal matters, such as paying bills, managing investments, or selling property. It remains in effect if the principal becomes incapacitated, ensuring that financial decisions continue to be managed without court intervention.

The DPOA covers financial and legal decisions, giving the agent control over managing assets, paying bills, and handling legal matters, while the MPOA is limited to healthcare decisions. The DPOA remains in effect if the principal becomes incapacitated, ensuring continuity in managing financial affairs, whereas the MPOA remains valid until it is revoked or until the principal regains the ability to make their own healthcare decisions.

Importance of Having Both DPOA and MPOA

Having both a Durable Power of Attorney (DPOA) and a Medical Power of Attorney (MPOA) or healthcare proxy is advisable for comprehensive estate planning. Advance directives give individuals control over their medical treatment and ensure that trusted agents or proxies can make decisions on their behalf. Combining a living will and a medical power of attorney or healthcare proxy provides a strong framework for making informed decisions about healthcare in critical situations. Similarly, having both a DPOA and MPOA guarantees that all aspects of your life—both medical and financial—are covered in the event of incapacity.

Creating an Advance Directive

It is understandable that no one wants to think about worst case scenarios like life support and serious medical intervention. The truth is, we have a lot less fear in situations we can control to some extent. Advance directives keep you in control, no matter what.

Setting up an advance healthcare directive is essential to guaranteeing that your medical wishes are respected if you become unable to make decisions for yourself. The process includes deciding what kind of care you want, appointing a trusted healthcare proxy, and drafting the necessary documents.

There are steps you must take when creating an advance healthcare directive.

First, you must decide what kinds of medical care you want to receive in an emergency. Think about the specific treatments you would or wouldn't want in life-threatening situations. These decisions may involve choices about life-sustaining treatments such as resuscitation (CPR), ventilators, or artificial nutrition. Be clear about your preferences so that your healthcare providers and proxy can act according to your wishes.

Next, you must determine who you want to act as your Healthcare Proxy. It goes without saying that you must choose someone you trust with your life, literally! This individual will be responsible for ensuring your medical wishes are carried out. Make sure they are willing to honor your preferences and can handle the responsibility. You'll need to formally name them in your **medical power of attorney (MPOA)** document.

Finally, you must draft the appropriate documents. You will need to draft two main documents: a **Living Will** and a **medical power of attorney (MPOA)**. These documents outline your medical preferences and designate someone to act on your behalf.

A **Living Will** specifies the types of medical treatments you would want or not want if you are incapacitated. It can seem scary to think about needing to prepare for such measures like a living will or advance directives, but this is actually an empowering process that gives you control over decisions in uncontrollable circumstances. There are four simple steps to creating your living will.

In step one, you will outline your treatment preferences. Specify treatments such as life support, resuscitation, ventilators, and feeding tubes. Decide in advance which treatments you would accept or refuse under various circumstances.

Step two involves establishing non-medical arrangements. Include personal preferences, such as spiritual care, pain management, or instructions on organ donation.

Step three is optional in case you wish to include guidelines for MPOA agents. If you have appointed a healthcare proxy, you can provide them with additional guidelines on how to make decisions for you.

Step four is where you will get witness and notary signatures for your documents. Once your living will is completed, you will need to sign it in the presence of witnesses or a notary, depending on your state's requirements, to make it legally binding.

The **medical power of attorney (MPOA)** appoints your health-care proxy, who will make decisions for you if you're unable to do so. Ensure that your proxy understands your preferences and is ready to make the tough decisions required.

In the **Appendices**, you'll find an **Incapacity Planning Toolkit** that includes downloadable forms and instructions for creating a **Living Will** and **medical power of attorney (MPOA)**. You can use these forms to ensure your advance directive complies with your state's legal requirements.

Once completed, it is important to distribute copies of your living will and healthcare proxy to your healthcare providers, family members, and anyone else involved in your care. This ensures that your wishes are accessible and followed during a medical emergency.

By taking these steps, you can create an effective advance directive that ensures your healthcare wishes are respected when you're unable to make decisions for yourself.

In this chapter, we covered the essential steps for creating advance directives, including a **living will** and **medical power of attorney (MPOA)**. These documents ensure that your healthcare preferences are honored and that a trusted person is empowered to make decisions on your behalf if you're unable to do so.

The key takeaway is the importance of preparing these documents early. Life is unpredictable, and having a living will and POA in place ensures that your wishes are respected in medical emergencies. Keeping these documents up-to-date is equally important, as your healthcare needs and preferences may change over time.

Once your documents are complete, share copies with your healthcare proxy and care providers. This will ensure that everyone involved is aware of your preferences and can act accordingly when necessary. By doing so, you provide peace of mind for yourself and your loved ones, reducing confusion or conflict during difficult times.

In the next chapter, we will explore **probate avoidance strategies** to further streamline the estate planning process and protect your assets.

Avoid Probate and Minimize Taxes

SEVEN

Probate Avoidance Strategies

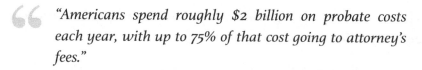

"Americans spend roughly $2 billion on probate costs each year, with up to 75% of that cost going to attorney's fees."

Source: Queens Probate Lawyer

U nderstanding how probate works—and more importantly, how to avoid it—can save individuals and their families a significant amount of money, time, and stress. Probate is the legal process through which a deceased person's estate is administered, but it often involves lengthy court procedures and high costs which can diminish the value of the estate. By implementing effective probate avoidance strategies, you can ensure that your assets are transferred directly to your loved ones without the delays and expenses associated with probate.

What Is Probate?

Probate is the legal process through which a deceased person's estate is distributed and settled according to their will or, if no will exists, according to state law. During probate, the court supervises the validation of the will, the payment of debts and taxes, and the distribution of remaining assets to the rightful beneficiaries.

Probate ensures that the assets of a deceased individual are properly distributed and any outstanding debts or taxes are settled. If there is a will, the executor named in the will oversees the distribution of assets under the supervision of the probate court. Without a will, the court appoints an administrator, and state laws dictate how assets are divided among surviving family members.

When a person dies leaving a valid will, the probate process generally follows these steps:

The will is filed with the probate court, and the executor named in the will is confirmed or appointed by the court.

All interested parties, including beneficiaries and creditors, are notified of the probate proceeding.

The executor compiles a list of the deceased's assets and values them.

Outstanding debts, taxes, and administrative expenses are paid from the estate.

Once debts and taxes are paid, the remaining assets are distributed to the beneficiaries as directed in the will.

If someone dies without a will (intestate), the probate process is slightly different. Since no executor is named, the court appoints an administrator to manage the estate. The administrator will need time to review documents and gather the necessary informa-tion. Heirs and creditors are notified, similar to the process with a will.

The administrator also takes stock of the estate's assets and values them. Debts and taxes are paid from the estate, just as in the process with a will. State intestacy laws determine how assets are distributed among surviving family members, often favoring spouses and children. Now that you have more insight into how much control can be given over to the court and their appointees when you do not have a written will, you can see why I have emphasized the importance of a complete estate plan.

There are some advantages and disadvantages of probate to consider.

Probate provides a structured, court-supervised process to ensure that the estate is settled according to legal standards, minimizing the risk of disputes or fraud. Probate also helps guarantee that all debts and taxes owed by the deceased are properly settled before assets are distributed.

However, it is important to understand that probate can be costly, with fees for court filings, attorneys, and executors often eating into the estate's value. As noted, attorney's fees can account for up to 75% of probate costs. It is also time consuming; probate can take months or even years to complete. This will delay the distribution of assets to your beneficiaries. Probate is also a public process, meaning that the details about the estate and its beneficiaries can be accessed by anyone, including creditors and the general public.

Factors Affecting Probate Length

There are a myriad of factors that affect how long probate can take. Knowing these factors ahead of planning your estate can help avoid the pitfalls that can prolong the process.

Understanding how probate works—and its potential drawbacks —highlights the importance of exploring strategies to avoid it whenever possible. The length of the probate process can vary greatly depending on several factors. Here's a look at the most common issues that can delay the settlement of an estate:

- **Wrong Executor/Trustee:** If the appointed executor is inexperienced, uncooperative, or unable to perform their duties, this can cause delays. A poorly chosen executor can lead to missed deadlines and prolonged court proceedings.
- **Absence of a Will:** When there's no will, the court must appoint an administrator, and the estate is distributed according to state intestacy laws. This can significantly extend the probate timeline as additional legal steps are required.
- **Asset Complexity:** Estates with complex assets, such as multiple properties, business interests, or unique financial instruments, require more time to evaluate and distribute.
- **Amount of Debts and Taxes:** Estates with substantial debts or tax obligations must go through additional steps to settle these, further prolonging the process. The estate may also need to file tax returns, adding to the time required.

- **Disputes Among Beneficiaries:** When beneficiaries disagree on the terms of the will or the distribution of assets, probate can become contentious, leading to legal challenges and delays.
- **Hard-to-Reach Beneficiaries:** If beneficiaries are difficult to locate, probate can be delayed while efforts are made to contact them. This can be especially problematic if beneficiaries reside in different countries.
- **Assets in Different States:** When a decedent owns property or assets in multiple states, each jurisdiction may require separate probate proceedings, further extending the process.
- **High Number of Beneficiaries:** More beneficiaries can mean more communication, potential disputes, and administrative tasks, all of which lengthen the probate process.
- **State Law:** Probate laws differ from state to state, and some jurisdictions have more streamlined processes than others. States with more complex probate procedures may require additional time to complete the process.

These factors illustrate why probate can sometimes be a lengthy and expensive process, reinforcing the importance of considering probate avoidance strategies. Overall, it is best to avoid probate when at all possible. A well written estate plan can help you do just that.

State-Specific Probate Laws

Paying attention to state specific probate laws is important when planning your estate. Probate laws vary from state to state, affecting the process, costs, and time it takes to settle an estate.

While each state has its unique rules, some states share similarities. Below is an overview of the probate laws for different states, highlighting commonalities where applicable.

The first group of states are those with simplified probate for small estates. Small estates under a certain value (ranging from $50,000 to $150,000) can use simplified probate. The process involves filing an affidavit or petition to transfer assets without court supervision.

Many states offer simplified probate procedures for small estates, allowing for a quicker and less expensive process. Typically, estates below a certain value can bypass full probate. These states include: **California, Texas, Florida, New York, Illinois, Pennsylvania, Ohio, Michigan, and Georgia.**

The second group of states are those with a Uniform Probate Code (UPC).

The **Uniform Probate Code (UPC)** is a set of standardized probate laws adopted by some states to streamline the process. States that follow the UPC often have more efficient procedures and allow for informal probate, which requires less court oversight. This group includes **Alaska, Arizona, Colorado, Hawaii, Idaho, Maine, Michigan, Minnesota, Montana, Nebraska, New Mexico, North Dakota, South Carolina, and Utah.** Informal probate allows for a less court-involved process, particularly if the estate is uncontested.

The third group of states includes those with Independent Administration.

Some states allow for independent administration of estates, where the executor has more freedom to manage and distribute assets without seeking court approval for each step. States included in this group are **Illinois, California, Texas, Nevada, and Indiana.** Independent administration means executors can handle most aspects of the estate, such as selling property or paying debts, without needing court approval at every stage.

The fourth group of states include those which require full probate for all estates.

In some states, all estates must go through full probate regardless of size, which can result in longer timelines and higher costs. This group includes **New York, New Jersey, Massachusetts, and Virginia.** Even small estates must go through the full probate process, which involves more court supervision and documentation. Thorough, precise planning will ease the process when the time comes for your estate to enter probate in these states.

Some states have additional considerations.

California offers simplified probate for small estates but has high probate fees that are a percentage of the estate's value.

Texas follows independent administration, which can help reduce court involvement, and allows for simplified probate for small estates.

Florida provides for summary administration if the estate is under $75,000 or the decedent has been dead for more than two years.

New York requires full probate for all estates, making it one of the more time-consuming and costly states for probate.

In the **Appendices**, you'll find a detailed table outlining **Probate Laws by State.** This includes important information such as small estate probate limits, whether the state follows the Uniform Probate Code (UPC), options for independent administration, and whether simplified probate procedures are available. This table will serve as a helpful resource to better understand probate processes in your specific state.

Each state's probate laws will impact how quickly and smoothly an estate is settled. For those interested in streamlining the process, understanding their state's specific requirements and exploring probate avoidance strategies is essential.

Probate Avoidance Strategies

No one wants to add complex legal stressors to the already difficult process of losing a loved one. Avoiding probate can save time, money, and stress for your heirs. Several strategies can help ensure that your assets pass directly to beneficiaries without going through court-supervised probate. Here's a look at some of the most effective probate avoidance strategies.

A **revocable living trust** is one of the most common and effective probate avoidance tools. In a living trust, you transfer ownership of your assets to the trust while still maintaining control over them during your lifetime. Upon your death, the assets in the trust are distributed to your beneficiaries without the need for probate. Since the trust is revocable, you can modify or revoke it at any time while you're alive. The benefits to a revocable living trust are that it avoids probate entirely, keeps estate matters private, allows for smooth asset management during life and after death. You create a trust document, name a trustee (who can be yourself during your lifetime), and transfer assets into the trust. Upon your death, the successor trustee distributes the assets according to your instructions.

Joint ownership of property allows for the automatic transfer of ownership to the surviving co-owner(s) upon your death. There are several types of joint ownership, but the most commonly used forms for probate avoidance are:

Joint Tenancy with Right of Survivorship: When one owner dies, the property automatically passes to the surviving joint tenant(s) without the need for probate.

Tenancy by the Entirety: Used for married couples, this form of joint ownership ensures that the property passes directly to the surviving spouse upon death.

Joint ownership helps avoid probate for the jointly owned asset—it is straightforward and easy to set up. You must title the asset (such as real estate or bank accounts) in both your name and the name of the co-owner as joint tenants with right of survivorship.

Giving away assets while you're still alive is another effective way to reduce the size of your estate and avoid probate. When you transfer ownership of an asset as a gift, it's no longer part of your estate, and therefore it bypasses probate. Giving away your assets reduces the taxable estate, simplifying the transfer process. You can gift up to the annual exclusion amount per individual each year (currently $17,000 in 2025) without incurring gift taxes. Gifts larger than this may require the filing of a gift tax return.

Pay-on-Death (POD) and **Transfer-on-Death (TOD)** designations are simple tools to transfer assets like bank accounts, retirement accounts, and securities directly to beneficiaries without probate. PODs are used for bank accounts. When you designate a beneficiary, the funds in the account automatically transfer to them upon your death. TODs are used for securities like stocks or bonds. The named beneficiary inherits the account without probate. These designations allow the direct and simple transfer of assets without the need for probate. You designate beneficiaries for each account with your financial institution, ensuring that the assets bypass probate and go directly to the named individuals.

Certain assets, such as life insurance policies, retirement accounts, and annuities allow you to name a **beneficiary** who will inherit the assets directly upon your death. These assets bypass probate entirely. They ensure a quick and direct transfer of assets to your designated beneficiary. When you open the account or purchase the policy, you name a beneficiary. It's important to review and update these designations regularly.

These probate avoidance strategies allow you to pass your assets to your loved ones quickly and with minimal expense. Creating a revocable living trust, utilizing joint ownership, making gifts, setting up POD or TOD accounts, and updating beneficiary designations are all effective ways to simplify estate administration and spare your heirs the costs and delays associated with probate.

This summary highlights the key aspects of probate, factors influencing its duration, and strategies to avoid it.

Now that we have explored the concept of probate, how it works, and the various factors that can affect its length and complexity, you are equipped to navigate planning around it. We also discussed key probate avoidance strategies such as creating a revocable living trust, joint ownership, gifting assets, and utilizing pay-on-death (POD) or transfer-on-death (TOD) accounts, as well as the importance of beneficiary designations. Understanding probate laws and applying these strategies can help streamline the estate settlement process, reducing costs, delays, and stress for your loved ones.

The key takeaway is that probate can be a lengthy and costly process, but with proper planning much of it can be avoided. Implementing strategies like trusts or POD/TOD accounts ensures that your assets are passed directly to your beneficiaries without going through probate.

It's important to consult with an estate planning attorney for personalized advice and guidance based on your specific situation and the probate laws in your state. Estate planning is not a one-time task; regularly reviewing and updating your estate plan ensures it reflects your current wishes and needs. If you engage an attorney, they can keep you up-to-date with any changes in the law that might affect your estate. But we will discuss attorneys and legal costs in detail in Chapter 9.

But before that, in the next chapter, we will explore **estate taxes** and how they can affect your estate planning. You are almost at the finish line learning how to plan your estate!

EIGHT

Estate Taxes and Tax Planning Strategies

As Benjamin Franklin famously said, "nothing is certain except death and taxes." Estate tax laws will vary based on a number of factors, including where you live and when your beneficiaries inherit your estate.

For 2025, the federal estate tax exemption is set at $13.61 million per individual, and for married couples the exemption is $27.22 million. This means that estates exceeding these values will be subject to federal estate taxes at rates ranging from 18% to 40%, depending on the taxable amount above the exemption. This higher exemption presents an opportunity for those with substantial estates to transfer significant wealth without being hit by estate taxes. However, it's important to note that this elevated exemption is scheduled to expire after 2025, at which point it could drop to around $5 million, adjusted for inflation.

Estate taxes are a significant concern for individuals with high net worth, and understanding how to minimize them is crucial for effective tax planning. With substantial estate values subject to high tax rates, it becomes essential to explore strategies that reduce the tax burden and preserve wealth for future generations. In this chapter, we will delve into estate taxes and the various planning strategies available to protect your assets.

What Is an Estate Tax?

Let's explore the concept and definition of estate taxes so you understand exactly how this plays a part in your planning. An **estate tax** is a federal or state tax levied on the transfer of a deceased person's estate before it is distributed to their heirs or beneficiaries. The estate tax is only applicable when the total value of the estate exceeds the exclusion limit set by law, and only the amount that exceeds this threshold is subject to taxation. Let's discuss how estate taxes work.

The **federal estate tax** is imposed on estates that exceed the federal exemption limit. In 2025, the federal estate tax exemption is $13.61 million for individuals and $27.22 million for married couples. If an estate exceeds this limit, the portion above the exemption is taxed at rates ranging from 18% to 40%.

For example, if an individual dies in 2025 with an estate worth $15 million, the taxable amount would be $15 million minus the $13.61 million exemption, or $1.39 million. The estate tax would then be applied only to that $1.39 million at the appropriate rate based on federal tax brackets.

Federal estate tax rates for 2025 range from 18% to 40%, with higher rates applying as the taxable amount increases.

In addition to federal estate taxes, some states levy their own estate taxes. However, state exemption thresholds vary, often being lower than the federal exemption.

Here are the states that impose estate taxes:

- **Connecticut:** Exemption is $13.61 million in 2025, subject to inflation adjustments.
- **Hawaii:** Exemption matches the federal exemption amount.
- **Illinois:** Estate tax kicks in for estates over $4 million.
- **Maine:** Exemption is $6.41 million.
- **Maryland:** Exemption is $5 million, but Maryland also has an inheritance tax.
- **Massachusetts:** Estate tax is applied to estates over $1 million.
- **Minnesota:** Exemption is $3 million.
- **New York:** Estate tax applies to estates over $6.58 million.
- **Oregon:** Exemption is $1 million.
- **Rhode Island:** Exemption is $1.73 million.
- **Vermont:** Exemption is $5 million.
- **Washington:** Exemption is $2.193 million.
- **District of Columbia:** Exemption is $4 million.

Each state has its own tax rates and exemption limits, so it is important for estate planners to understand their specific state's rules to minimize the tax impact.

An **inheritance tax** is different from an estate tax in that it is paid by the beneficiaries who inherit the assets, rather than by the estate itself. Only a few states levy inheritance taxes, and the rates may vary depending on the beneficiary's relationship to the deceased. Close relatives like spouses are often exempt from this tax. Here is the break down:

State	Tax Rate (%)	Exemptions for Spouses	Exemptions for Children	Exemptions for Other Relatives	Exemptions for Non-relatives
Iowa	Up to 15%	Yes	Yes	Reduced rates for siblings, exempt for other close relatives	Full tax applies
Kentucky	Up to 16%	Yes	Yes	Reduced rates for siblings, higher rates for others	Full tax applies
Maryland	Up to 10%	Yes	Up to $5,000	Up to $5,000 exemption, higher rates for others	Full tax applies after $1,000 exemption
Nebraska	Up to 18%	Yes	Yes	Reduced rates for siblings, higher rates for others	Full tax applies
New Jersey	Up to 16%	Yes	Yes	Reduced rates for siblings, higher rates for others	Full tax applies
Pennsylvania	Up to 15%	Yes	Yes	Reduced rates for siblings, higher rates for others	Full tax applies

To calculate the estate tax liability, follow these four simple steps.

Determine Your Gross Estate

This includes all assets, such as real estate, bank accounts, investments, retirement accounts, and life insurance policies.

Subtract Deductions

Deductions include outstanding debts, funeral expenses, administrative costs, and mortgages.

Consider Charitable Deductions or Transfers to Spouse

Assets transferred to a spouse or donated to charity are generally tax-exempt.

Find Your Tax Liability

After applying deductions, subtract the estate tax exemption limit from the remaining estate value. The excess amount is taxed according to federal and state estate tax rates.

By understanding how federal and state estate taxes work and planning accordingly, individuals can minimize their estate's tax burden and preserve more of their assets for their beneficiaries.

Strategies to Minimize Estate Taxes

Taxes are inevitable, but there are strategies to mitigate their impact on your beneficiaries. Minimizing estate taxes is key to ensuring that more of your assets pass to your heirs instead of being used to pay taxes. Below are some of the most effective strategies, accompanied by real-world examples to clarify their application. As you read these descriptions, make a note of which examples best apply to your own circumstances.

Unlimited transfers can be made between spouses during life or at death without incurring estate taxes, using the unlimited marital deduction.

For example, If John dies in 2025 and leaves his $15 million estate to his wife, Sarah, the entire amount transfers tax-free due to the marital deduction. This defers any estate tax until Sarah passes away, at which point her estate will be subject to taxation based on the exemption amount at that time.

By **making lifetime gifts to children or grandchildren**, you can reduce the value of your estate. In 2025, individuals can give up to $19,000 per person annually without incurring gift taxes (this is the annual gift tax exclusion).

Consider the following scenario. Emily gifts $19,000 to each of her three children and two grandchildren. This totals $95,000 in one year, reducing the size of her taxable estate and keeping it under the taxable limit.

Setting up **trusts or custodial accounts for minors** (such as UGMA/UTMA accounts) allows for tax-free gifts under the annual gift exclusion.

Let's say Robert gifts $50,000 to a custodial account for his nephew, who is a minor. By the time his nephew reaches adulthood, the account has grown, and Robert has reduced his estate's value without incurring taxes on the gift.

AB Trusts are split into two trusts: one for the surviving spouse and one for heirs. **QTIP Trusts** provide income to the surviving spouse, with the remaining assets passing to heirs upon the spouse's death, delaying estate taxes.

Let's take a look at an example. When Sarah dies, her estate is valued at $20 million. An **AB Trust** is created, splitting the estate between Trust A for her husband, and Trust B for her heirs. Trust B benefits from Sarah's estate tax exemption, deferring taxes on Trust A until her husband's death.

A **Family Limited Partnership** (FLP)allows you to transfer assets to family members while maintaining control, effectively lowering the taxable value.

Here is one instance of family limited partnership. The Davis family creates an FLP for their real estate holdings. They transfer ownership of the properties to the FLP, allowing them to gift shares to their children at a discounted value, reducing the overall estate size.

A **private annuity** involves transferring assets to heirs in exchange for a lifetime annuity, removing the assets from your estate.

Imagine this scenario: Michael transfers $3 million to his daughter in exchange for lifetime annuity payments. Upon his death, the assets are no longer part of his estate, avoiding taxes on that entire amount of $3 million!

You may want to consider a **special use real estate valuation.** This strategy allows for reduced property valuation based on its current use rather than market value, which can apply to agricultural or business properties.

One example of this strategy is found in the case of Sandra. Sandra's family farm is worth $4 million. However, using special use valuation for estate tax purposes, the value is reduced to $2.5 million due to its agricultural use, significantly lowering the tax bill.

A **Qualified Personal Residence Trust, or QPRT,** allows you to transfer your home into a trust while continuing to live there for a specified period, reducing the taxable value of the home.

Let's say David transfers his $2 million home into a QPRT for his children. He continues to live there for 10 years, after which the house is passed to his children, reducing the estate's taxable value by the home's appreciation during that period.

Charitable trusts remove assets from the estate, reducing its taxable value. **Charitable remainder trusts (CRTs)** provide lifetime income, with the remainder going to charity after death.

For example, Sarah transfers $1 million into a CRT, providing her with income during her life and transferring the remainder to her favorite charity. This removes the $1 million from her taxable estate.

Contributions to **'529' plans or custodial accounts** for education reduce the estate's value, qualifying for the annual gift tax exclusion.

Consider the following case. John contributes $75,000 to a 529 college savings plan for his granddaughter. He uses the five-year gift tax averaging option, removing the amount from his taxable estate without triggering gift taxes.

An **Irrevocable Life Insurance Trust, or ILIT,** keeps life insurance proceeds out of your taxable estate. You transfer ownership of a life insurance policy to a trust. Since the trust owns the policy, its death benefit is excluded from your taxable estate.

For example, Helen owns a $5 million life insurance policy. Without an ILIT, the payout would be included in her estate, subjecting it to taxes. By placing the policy in an ILIT, the $5 million is excluded, avoiding estate taxes.

Now that you have had a chance to learn about the different types of tax reduction strategies and gotten acquainted with real-world examples, you have a better idea of how to plan. Remember to plan for life changes, such as the birth of grandchildren, to accommodate your long term estate planning.

By combining several of these strategies, individuals can significantly reduce the size of their taxable estate and may be even avoid estate taxes altogether.

Understanding Unified Credit, Estate Tax Exemption, and Estate Tax Return

Now that we have covered the fundamentals of estate taxes, let's cover unified tax credits.

The **unified tax credit** is a dollar amount that an individual can use to offset estate and gift taxes, effectively reducing their tax liability. This credit unifies the estate tax and gift tax into a single system. It means that any amount gifted during a person's lifetime or passed on after death can be applied toward the unified credit before taxes are owed.

How It Works: The IRS sets an exemption limit for gifts and estates combined. For example, the **unified tax credit** in 2025 allows individuals to pass on up to $13.99 million in lifetime gifts and estate transfers without incurring federal gift or estate taxes.

Each dollar gifted during your lifetime counts against the unified credit, meaning you must carefully balance lifetime gifting and post-death estate planning.

Example: If you give $1 million as a gift during your lifetime, the remaining credit for estate transfers would be reduced by that amount. If your estate is worth $10 million when you pass, only $9 million would be exempt from taxes.

The **estate tax exemption** is the amount of money or assets that can be passed to heirs without being subject to federal estate taxes. For 2025, the estate tax exemption is $13.61 million for individuals and $27.22 million for married couples.

Any amount exceeding this exemption is taxed at rates ranging from 18% to 40%.

Here's a quick breakdown of how estate taxes apply based on different brackets:

Taxable Amount	Estate Tax Rate	Base Tax	What You Pay
$0 to $10,000	0,18	$0	18% on the taxable amount
$10,001 to $20,000	0,2	$1,800	$1,800 + 20% on the taxable amount over $10,000
$20,001 to $40,000	0,22	$3,800	$3,800 + 22% on the taxable amount over $20,000
$40,001 to $60,000	0,24	$8,200	$8,200 + 24% on the taxable amount over $40,000
$60,001 to $80,000	0,26	$13,000	$13,000 + 26% on the taxable amount over $60,000
$80,001 to $100,000	0,28	$18,200	$18,200 + 28% on the taxable amount over $80,000
$100,001 to $150,000	0,3	$23,800	$23,800 + 30% on the taxable amount over $100,000
$150,001 to $250,000	0,32	$38,800	$38,800 + 32% on the taxable amount over $150,000
$250,001 to $500,000	0,34	$70,800	$70,800 + 34% on the taxable amount over $250,000
$500,001 to $750,000	0,37	$155,800	$155,800 + 37% on the taxable amount over $500,000
$750,001 to $1 million	0,39	$248,300	$248,300 + 39% on the taxable amount over $750,000
Over $1 million	0,4	$345,800	$345,800 + 40% on the taxable amount over $1 million

The base tax is a fixed amount you pay for each estate tax bracket before applying the percentage rate to the taxable amount that exceeds the lower end of the bracket. For example, if the taxable estate is $25,000, the base tax for the $20,001–$40,000 bracket is $3,800. You would then pay an additional 22% on the amount over $20,000, in this case, $5,000. This ensures that taxes are progressively applied, with each higher tax bracket adding a base tax to the total.

Gift Tax: The gift tax applies to any transfer of wealth during a person's lifetime. You can gift up to $19,000 per recipient in 2025 without triggering the gift tax. Lifetime gifts exceeding the annual exclusion count against the unified credit.

Generation-Skipping Transfer Tax (GSTT): This tax applies to transfers made to grandchildren or individuals more than one generation younger than the donor. The GSTT is designed to prevent families from avoiding estate taxes by skipping a generation.

By utilizing the **unified tax credit, estate tax exemptions,** and understanding related taxes like the **gift tax** and **generation-skipping tax,** individuals can craft a strategic estate plan that reduces the overall tax burden for their heirs.

State-Specific Tax Laws

Where you live can have a significant impact on how your estate and heirs are taxed. The following information offers insight into how your state taxes will apply. Remember: as time passes, laws can change. It is important to stay up-to-date on legal changes in your state and adjust your plan accordingly to make sure your best interests are covered.

Estate and inheritance tax laws vary by state, with only a few states still imposing these taxes. Here's a breakdown of state-specific estate and inheritance taxes:

States with Estate Taxes:

- **Connecticut:** The top estate tax rate is 12% for estates exceeding $13.61 million.
- **Hawaii:** Estates over $5.49 million are subject to a top tax rate of 20%.
- **Illinois:** Estates valued above $4 million are taxed at a rate up to 16%.
- **Maine:** The estate tax rate ranges from 8% to 12% for estates exceeding $6.41 million.
- **Maryland:** The top estate tax rate is 16%, applicable to estates exceeding $5 million.
- **Massachusetts:** Estates over $1 million face a top tax rate of 16%.
- **Minnesota:** Estates valued above $3 million are taxed at rates up to 16%.
- **New York:** Estates exceeding $6.58 million are subject to a 16% tax.
- **Oregon:** The estate tax rate is 16% for estates over $1 million.
- **Rhode Island:** Estates exceeding $1.73 million are taxed at up to 16%.
- **Vermont:** The estate tax applies to estates above $5 million, with rates up to 16%.
- **Washington:** The estate tax rate is 20% for estates over $2.193 million.
- **District of Columbia:** The estate tax is 20% for estates exceeding $4.528 million.
- States with Inheritance Taxes:
- **Iowa:** The inheritance tax rate is up to 6%, with no exemption threshold.

- **Kentucky:** Inheritance tax rates range from 4% to 16%, depending on the heir's relationship to the deceased.
- **Maryland:** In addition to estate tax, there is a 10% inheritance tax.
- **Nebraska:** Inheritance tax rates vary, with a maximum of 15% for certain heirs.
- **New Jersey:** The inheritance tax ranges from 11% to 16%, depending on the value of the estate and the relationship of the heir.

It's important to note that some states, like Maryland, impose both estate and inheritance taxes. If you live in a state with these taxes, it's crucial to understand how they work. You might also consult an estate attorney for guidance.

For a complete breakdown of **State-Specific Estate and Inheritance Taxes,** please refer to the detailed table located in the **Appendices.**

Filing an Estate Tax Return

An **estate tax return** is a legal document that must be filed with the government after an individual's death to report the total value of their estate, including all assets and liabilities. The purpose of this return is to calculate any estate taxes that may be due based on the estate's net value, current tax rates, and exemptions in place at the time of death.

There are six simple steps you need to follow for filing an Estate Tax Return, also known as Form 706.

First, you must determine if you need to file Form 706.

Form 706 must be filed if the total value of the decedent's estate exceeds the estate tax exemption limit. In 2025, the federal estate tax exemption is $13.61 million. If the estate's value is above this threshold, filing Form 706 is required.

Second, you need to obtain the necessary forms.

Download **IRS Form 706** and its instructions, which are available in this book, on the IRS website or through your estate attorney. This form reports the estate's value and calculates the amount of tax owed.

Third, you will gather your documentation.

Collect all relevant documents related to the estate, including property titles, bank accounts, retirement accounts, life insurance policies, and appraisals for real estate and personal property.

Fourth, you complete the form.

Accurately enter the values for all assets and liabilities in the estate, and apply any deductions or credits. The deductions may include funeral expenses, debts, charitable donations, and transfers to a surviving spouse.

Fifth, you will need to file the form.

Form 706 must be filed within nine months of the decedent's death. Extensions can be requested by filing **Form 4768** for an additional six months if needed.

Sixth, you will pay any taxes due.

After calculating the estate tax liability, arrange for payment of any taxes due. Payments can be made directly to the IRS using the details provided in the instructions for Form 706.

Form 706 should be filed by the executor or personal representative of the estate. In cases where no executor is appointed, the responsibility falls to any person in actual or constructive possession of the estate's assets.

You will want to avoid these common issues with Form 706. First, you do not want to miss the filing deadline. Failing to file the return within the required nine months can result in penalties and interest. If more time is needed, it's important to file **Form 4768** to request an extension. Second, you want to make sure you provide adequate documentation. Providing incomplete or inaccurate information can delay the return process or trigger an IRS audit. It is crucial to include detailed documentation, such as property appraisals and financial records.

Sample Documents

- **Form 706:** Sample Form 706
- **Instructions for Form 706:** Instructions for Form 706

By ensuring all steps are followed carefully, the estate's tax liability can be calculated correctly and filed without issues. Estate planners and executors should consider consulting with a tax professional or attorney to avoid mistakes in the filing process.

In this chapter, we explored the process of filing an estate tax return, specifically focusing on the importance of accurately reporting the value of an estate using IRS Form 706. Properly filing the estate tax return is essential to ensure that the estate's tax liability is calculated correctly and that any owed taxes are paid on time. The key takeaway is the necessity of thorough documentation, timely filing, and a clear understanding of estate tax laws.

Estate tax planning can be complex, and it's crucial to seek professional guidance to navigate the intricacies and avoid common mistakes. Engaging with an estate attorney or tax advisor ensures that your estate plan is compliant with the law and optimized to minimize tax burdens. But how might seeking legal counsel affect your estate planning and the costs associated with it?

In the next chapter, we will cover legal costs and common pitfalls in estate planning to help you further refine your estate planning strategies. You have learned a lot already about how to strategically optimize your estate and reduce taxes for your heirs. You should be feeling pretty confident about your ability to navigate the process by now. Let's keep learning together so you are fully equipped to plan your estate.

Consider Costs and Legal Pitfalls

NINE

Legal Fees and Pitfalls

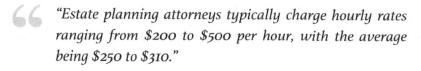 *"Estate planning attorneys typically charge hourly rates ranging from $200 to $500 per hour, with the average being $250 to $310."*

Source: Finance Strategists

L egal fees can significantly affect the overall cost of creating an estate plan. The more complex your estate, the more time it will take, which means higher costs. It's important to understand these fees upfront so you can plan accordingly.

Beyond legal fees, there are also common mistakes people make when setting up their estate plans. This chapter will go over the types of legal fees you might encounter and the common issues you should avoid. This will help you approach your estate planning process with a clear understanding of potential costs and risks. This is essentially a cost-benefit equation: what kind of benefit are you receiving by spending on attorneys? You should be able to answer this question for yourself by the end of this chapter.

Understanding Legal Costs

The cost of estate planning can vary significantly depending on several factors. You will want to consider these factors to determine what influences your costs.

You want to consider the complexity of the estate. If your estate is straightforward with few assets and no complicated legal issues, the cost will generally be lower. Estates with multiple assets, business ownership, or potential disputes among heirs often require more time and expertise, increasing legal fees.

Legal fees may be charged at hourly or flat rates. Estate planning attorneys typically charge between $200 and $500 per hour, depending on their experience and state in which they practice. Some attorneys may offer flat fees for specific services, such as drafting a will or trust. Attorneys with specialized knowledge or more years of experience may charge higher rates, but they may also be more efficient and better equipped to handle complex estates.

Geographical location will be a factor in cost determination. Estate planning costs can vary based on where you live. Urban areas or regions with higher costs of living may have higher legal fees.

The number of documents and the types of documents required to plan your estate, including what might constitute primary documents in your case, will be the most important factor in determining your legal fees. These documents might include wills, trusts, and powers of attorney. Remember to factor in ongoing costs. Estate plans often require maintenance and updates over time, especially when laws change or your personal circumstances evolve. These updates come with additional costs.

Breakdown of Typical Estate Planning Costs:

- **Simple Will:** $150 to $500
- **Living Trust:** $1,000 to $2,500
- **Power of Attorney:** $200 to $500
- **Healthcare Directives:** $100 to $500
- **Comprehensive Estate Plan:** $2,500 to $5,000 or more, depending on complexity.

For example, if you have a simple estate and only need a basic will and power of attorney, your costs may stay below $1,000. However, a more complex estate plan with multiple trusts and ongoing management could easily exceed $5,000. Understanding these factors will help you plan for the financial side of estate planning.

Choosing the Right Attorney

Choosing the right attorney for your estate plan is important to make sure your wishes are documented and carried out correctly. Here are some straightforward tips to help you through the process.

Start by asking the right questions when you meet with a potential attorney:

- Is estate planning your main focus?
- How long have you been practicing?
- Do you handle the entire process, or does someone else take over at some point?
- Do you review estate plans periodically?

- What's your experience with estate taxes?
- Can you create a full plan with wills, trusts, and life insurance?
- How do you charge—hourly or a flat rate?
- What's your view on revocable living trusts?
- Will you let me review documents before finalizing?
- Does your firm ever act as trustee or executor?
- Will someone be available to answer my questions if you're not available?

You should also think about how comfortable you feel with the attorney:

- Are they clear and easy to understand?
- Do you share the same general values?
- Do you feel you can talk to them about personal matters?

When choosing an attorney, don't just go by location.

- Get a referral from another attorney or advisor you trust.
- Be cautious with internet directories—they may not provide enough details.
- Make sure the attorney has malpractice insurance.
- Check their reputation and client reviews.
- See if they are available and responsive when needed.

Choosing the right attorney is a serious responsibility. While all estate planning attorneys may possess similar credentials, you should also feel good about whom you hire. Following these tips will help you find an attorney who's the right fit for your estate planning needs.

Common Pitfalls

When creating an estate plan, there are several common pitfalls that people often overlook. Avoiding these mistakes can help ensure your estate plan works the way you intend. Here are some key issues to watch out for:

Avoiding to name contingent beneficiaries can be an issue. Always have backup beneficiaries in case the primary ones can't or don't want to accept the inheritance.

Not planning for disability or nursing home care is a common pitfall. Failing to plan for potential disability can leave important decisions about your care and finances in the hands of the court instead of a trusted individual. Without a plan for long-term care, the costs could quickly eat into your estate. Pre-planning for nursing home or assisted living care can protect your assets.

Putting your child's name on the deed to your home is a mistake. Adding your child to the deed of your home can create complications, such as triggering gift taxes or making the home vulnerable to your child's creditors.

Choosing the wrong person to handle your estate will have major consequences. Selecting an executor or trustee who isn't up to the task can lead to delays, mistakes, or even family conflicts.

Not transferring your life insurance policies to a life insurance trust is another common pitfall. If your life insurance policies are not transferred to an irrevocable life insurance trust (ILIT), the proceeds may be subject to estate taxes.

Not making gifts to reduce estate tax will cost you. Making gifts during your lifetime can reduce the size of your taxable estate and potentially lower estate tax liability.

Changes in state residency impacts your costs and planning.
Moving to another state can affect your estate plan, as laws differ
from state to state. It's important to update your plan if you change
your primary residence.

Fulfilling philanthropic goals *without a plan* might derail them.
If you have charitable intentions, not including a clear plan in
your estate could result in your philanthropic goals not being met.

By keeping these pitfalls in mind and avoiding them, you can
create a more effective and well-rounded estate plan.

DIY Estate Planning

DIY estate planning is the process of creating your estate plan
using online templates or services without the help of an attorney.
This approach can seem appealing because it's often cheaper and
more accessible, but it also comes with certain risks.

There are some pros to DIY Estate Planning to consider. It is
extremely cost effective and convenient. You can complete a DIY
estate plan at your own pace, from the comfort of your home,
without needing to schedule appointments or meeting with an
attorney. Often this option is free or low cost with the help of a
simple template. For individuals with very simple estates—
minimal assets, no children, and no complex legal or tax issues—
DIY estate planning might provide a basic, workable solution.

There are also some cons associated with DIY Estate Planning to
consider. One of the biggest drawbacks of DIY estate planning is
the absence of professional legal advice. This can lead to mistakes,
missed opportunities, and incomplete documents. DIY estate
plans may not fully account for state-specific laws or tax issues,
leading to unintended consequences, like higher estate taxes or

probate complications. If your estate involves multiple assets, trusts, business interests, or special family circumstances, DIY estate planning can easily become inadequate or problematic. Without proper legal oversight, documents may be incomplete, improperly executed, or invalid under state law.

This book includes many concrete templates that you can use to get started on your estate plan. *However, keep in mind that even one small mistake can invalidate these documents.* It's always a good idea to have your documents reviewed by an estate planning attorney so that you have the peace of mind that they are legally sound and meet all your needs.

Minimizing Overall Legal Costs

Estate planning can be expensive, but there are several ways to reduce legal fees while still ensuring your plan is solid and effective. Here are some strategies to help minimize costs:

Be Prepared. Before meeting with an attorney, gather all relevant financial documents and have a clear idea of your goals. Being organized and prepared can save time and reduce the number of hours you'll need to pay for.

Shop Around. Compare rates from different estate planning attorneys to ensure that you're getting the best value. Look for attorneys who specialize in estate planning, but don't hesitate to ask about fees upfront and what services are included.

Use Templates for Simple Wills. If your estate is straightforward, you may be able to use templates for simple wills and other basic documents. This book provides many templates that you can start with, though it's still important to have them reviewed by a professional.

Keep it Simple. Avoid overcomplicating your estate plan. The more complex your plan is, the more time and legal expertise it will require, which drives up costs. Stick to the essentials and streamline where possible.

By following these strategies, you can effectively manage the cost of estate planning without sacrificing quality.

In this chapter, we explored the costs associated with estate planning and how to minimize them. The key takeaway is that while estate planning can be costly, there are ways to manage these expenses by being prepared, using templates for simple documents, and keeping the process straightforward. However, it's crucial to remember that estate planning is complex, and seeking professional legal advice is important to avoid costly mistakes.

Before deciding on DIY estate planning or hiring an attorney, carefully weigh your options. Each estate is unique, and a personalized approach is essential for ensuring that your wishes are carried out properly.

In the next chapter, we will cover how to maintain and update your estate plan, ensuring that it continues to reflect your current wishes and legal requirements. You are now ready for the final steps in creating your estate plan.

Yearly Review and Maintenance

TEN

Maintaining and Reviewing Your Estate Plan

"There's nothing fun about stuff like estate planning, getting mammograms, or talking to a guy about long-term disability insurance, but you do it anyway. Trust me, the stress of not having done the above is prematurely aging."

Jen Lancaster

Reviewing and updating your estate plan may not be enjoyable, but it's something you need to do to make sure everything is in order. By regularly updating your plan, you'll know that your final wishes will be followed. This is the peace of mind that rewards your temporary hard work for the long term.

Life changes, and so do laws, so keeping your estate plan up to date ensures that things like new family members, changes in assets, or legal updates are covered. In this chapter, we'll talk about when and how to review your plan and the steps you need to take to keep it current. Let's dive into it together.

Why and When to Review Your Estate Plan

It's important to review your estate plan regularly to make sure it still fits your current situation and wishes. Here are some key reasons why you might need to update it:

Family changes such as the birth or adoption of a child will require you to update your estate plan to include guardianship and inheritance details. The same applies to a marriage, divorce or the death of a family member. Changes in marital status can affect your beneficiaries and how your assets are divided. If a beneficiary or executor passes away, you will need to make adjustments to your plan.

Health changes such as serious illness or disability for you or a loved one might require updates to your healthcare directives or powers of attorney. If you anticipate long term care, it is important to plan for these costs and how to manage them.

Work changes such as a new job or promotion, retirement, or business ownership can impact your income or benefits. You need to make updates which reflect these changes to your estate plan.

Market changes can impact your asset values. If the value of your assets has significantly changed, you'll want to make sure your estate plan accounts for those fluctuations. Adjusting your plan during economic shifts can help protect your assets.

Changes to the law will impact your estate plan and require adjustment to your documents. If there's been a change in tax laws, such as exemption limits, you may need to adjust your estate plan to reduce tax liabilities. Changes in estate planning laws might require you to update your documents. Healthcare laws might change, requiring you to update your directives.

By now you are probably wondering how often you should review your estate plan. Here are some guidelines to consider. If there haven't been any major changes in your life—like marriage, divorce, the birth of a child, a death in the family, a job change, or changes in your assets—it's still a good idea to review your estate plan every **five years**. Regular reviews will help keep everything up to date and make sure your wishes are still being met.

In short, keeping your estate plan updated is crucial to ensuring that everything is handled the way you want. Regular reviews will make sure your plan stays relevant to your life and the law.

How to Update Your Estate Plan

Updating your estate plan is an important process that reflects your latest wishes, and it helps avoid complications down the line. Failing to update your plan can lead to unintended consequences, such as outdated beneficiaries, improper asset distribution, or tax issues. Here's a guide to updating your estate plan and why it's necessary.

Remember, it is vital that you update your plan as often as these changes occur. If you don't keep your estate plan current, you run the risk of having an outdated document that no longer reflects your intentions. This could mean:

Outdated beneficiaries: Your assets may go to someone you no longer wish to include.

Inaccurate asset distribution: Changes in your assets or finances might not be reflected, leading to unequal or unintended distributions.

Tax implications: New tax laws could result in higher taxes if your plan isn't updated.

Legal complications: Outdated estate plans may not comply with current laws, causing issues during probate.

Follow these simple steps for updating your estate plan.

Review your current Estate Plan. Start by looking over your existing documents. Identify any areas that may need to be updated, such as beneficiary designations or asset allocations. Check if there are any gaps that need to be addressed.

Consider life and financial changes. Reflect on any major life changes like marriage, divorce, the birth of a child, or a significant shift in your financial situation. These changes are key triggers for updating your estate plan.

Take another round of asset inventory. Conduct a fresh review of your assets, including property, investments, and other financial holdings. This will help you decide how you want to allocate these assets in your updated plan.

Revise your legal documents. Work with an attorney to update your legal documents, such as wills, trusts, and powers of attorney. Ensure that everything aligns with your current life situation, financial state, and legal requirements.

By following these steps, you can keep your estate plan up-to-date and avoid potential problems in the future. Regular updates make sure that your wishes are carried out the way you intend and help minimize any legal or financial issues for your loved ones. You don't want to put in the time and cost of estate planning only to have it fall apart because you did not update as needed.

Reinforcing the Roles of Your Executor and Trustee

Let's reinforce the roles of your executor and trustee. The **executor** plays a critical role in managing your estate after you pass away. Their primary responsibility is to ensure that your final wishes, as outlined in your will, are carried out correctly. Here are the main duties of an executor:

Managing the estate: The executor is responsible for gathering and managing the assets of the estate.

Paying debts and taxes: They must settle any outstanding debts or taxes owed by the estate.

Distributing assets: The executor distributes the estate's assets to the beneficiaries according to the terms of the will.

Handling legal processes: This includes filing necessary paperwork, representing the estate in court, and overseeing the probate process.

Choosing the right executor is important to ensure that your estate is managed smoothly and in accordance with your wishes. While this might sound complex, it really isn't. Here are some tips:

Choose someone you trust. The executor should be someone you trust to manage your assets and carry out your wishes.

Ask first. Make sure the person is willing to take on the role before naming them as your executor.

Get back up. Consider naming an alternate executor in case the first person is unable to fulfill the role.

Consider their qualifications. Select someone with the skills to manage finances and handle the responsibilities of settling your estate.

Get professional advice. You can consult a legal professional to guide you in choosing the right executor.

Keep it close to home. It's often helpful to choose someone who lives nearby to make managing the estate more practical. However, this should not be done at the expense of trust.

Respect their age. Choose someone who is likely to be around and capable when the time comes to carry out their duties.

Review your options. Periodically revisit your choice of executor to ensure that they are still the best fit.

Consider legal guidelines. Be aware of any local laws or regulations that might impact your choice of executor.

Check in with your executor regularly. It's important to approach your executor periodically to ensure that they are still willing and able to manage your estate. Circumstances can change, and they might have a change of heart or face new personal challenges.

A trustee manages the assets held in a trust and ensures that the terms of the trust are followed. Like an executor, the trustee has a legal responsibility to act in the best interest of the beneficiaries and the estate. Understanding their role helps you choose the right person for the job. Here are the key duties of a trustee:

Managing trust assets: The trustee oversees investments, property, and any other assets placed in the trust.

Distributing income and assets: They distribute income or assets to the beneficiaries as specified in the trust agreement.

Filing taxes: Trustees are responsible for handling the tax returns for the trust.

Fiduciary responsibility: A trustee must always act in the best interests of the beneficiaries, managing the trust with care and loyalty.

Selecting the right trustee ensures that your assets are handled appropriately and that the trust is properly managed. Choose someone who is trustworthy and reliable, as they will be managing your assets on behalf of your beneficiaries. It's helpful to select a trustee who has some experience or knowledge in handling finances or legal matters.

A trustee should be able to communicate effectively with the beneficiaries and other involved parties. It is important they are able to remain neutral and avoid any conflicts of interest, especially if family dynamics are involved. Since a trust can last for many years, consider choosing someone who is likely to be around to fulfill their duties long-term. If you feel that none of your personal connections are suited for the job, you can opt for a professional trustee, such as a bank or trust company. By carefully selecting the right executor and trustee, you can ensure that your estate and assets are managed according to your wishes, minimizing the risk of disputes and errors.

Customizing your Estate Plan

Estate planning is not a one-size-fits-all process, and each situation requires careful consideration to ensure your wishes are carried out. Here are some key considerations for specific family dynamics. Whether some or all of these circumstances apply to your own estate plan, it is a good idea to have a grasp on each of them since life changes as we live it.

Blended families have unique estate planning needs.

Estate planning for blended families can be more complicated than for traditional families. A **blended family** typically includes a couple where one or both partners have children from previous relationships. Planning in this case requires extra care to ensure your spouse and children from different relationships are all taken care of, and potential conflicts are minimized.

In blended families, the process is more complex because you need to balance the needs of your current spouse and your children from prior relationships. If you don't plan carefully, your spouse could end up inheriting most of your assets, leaving your children from a previous marriage with little or nothing. On the other hand, leaving everything to your children could leave your spouse financially vulnerable.

A blended family can include couples where one or both spouses have children from previous relationships, or families that have both biological and stepchildren. Each of these situations requires thoughtful estate planning to make sure everyone's interests are covered.

Here are some effective tools for planning your estate in a blended family:

Family Trusts: A family trust allows you to control how your assets are used by your spouse and children. You can set it up so your spouse has access to the assets during their lifetime, and the remaining assets go to your children when your spouse passes away.

Marital Trusts (QTIP Trusts): This type of trust provides for your spouse while ensuring that after they pass, the remaining assets go to your children. It helps protect both your spouse and children.

Outright Ownership: You can choose to leave certain assets directly to your spouse or children. However, this can cause conflicts if you worry about your spouse not distributing assets to your children after their death.

Immediate Bequests: You can leave specific assets directly to your children or heirs upon your death, making sure they receive their inheritance without any delays.

Here are some important things to keep in mind when creating an estate plan for a blended family:

Consider the possibility of remarriage. While it might not seem like something you need to consider, the reality is that many people remarry after losing their partner. You are simply planning for all possibilities of life. If your spouse remarries after your death, it could affect how your assets are distributed. You can include provisions to prevent this from impacting your children's inheritance.

You might need more than a will. A will may not be enough for a blended family. Trusts can offer better protection and ensure assets are distributed according to your wishes.

Communication is important. Discuss your estate plan openly with your spouse and children to avoid surprises or conflicts later on.

Regularly review beneficiary designations. Life changes, so make sure to update your beneficiary designations on life insurance policies, retirement accounts, and other financial products.

Decide who will make decisions in the event you become incapacitated. Set up a power of attorney and healthcare proxy to ensure someone you trust is in charge of your finances and healthcare decisions if you become incapacitated.

Consider prenuptial agreements. If you're in a second or later marriage, consider a prenuptial or postnuptial agreement to clarify how assets should be divided, which can help avoid conflicts later.

Estate planning for blended families requires careful thought to make sure your spouse and children from previous relationships are all taken care of in a fair way so as to minimize the possibility of intra-family disputes arising in the immediate aftermath of your death. Trusts, regular reviews of your plan, and clear communication with your family can help prevent disputes and make sure your wishes are respected. It's also a good idea to consult with an estate planning attorney to make sure your plan is thorough and effective.

Estate planning is equally important for single individuals as it is for couples or families. Without a spouse or partner automatically taking charge of your assets or decision-making, it's vital to ensure that your wishes are clear and legally binding. Singles need to be proactive in estate planning to avoid unintended consequences. Here's a guide on how to approach estate planning as a single individual.

For **single people**, estate planning requires more attention to detail since there may be no automatic next of kin to handle your affairs. If you don't make your wishes known, intestate laws (which govern what happens if someone dies without a will) could dictate how your assets are divided. This might not align with your personal preferences, as these laws usually favor blood relatives.

Additionally, single individuals must consider who will make medical and financial decisions on their behalf if they become incapacitated, as there's no spouse to fill this role by default. As a single person, you want to make sure you know who will be making decisions on your behalf if you are unable to do so.

Here are some key estate planning tools and strategies that single people should consider. We have discussed many of these before, but as we approach the end of the book, it is essential to revise some of the essential lessons in estate planning.

Wills and Trusts: Creating a will is the most basic step in estate planning. It lets you decide who will inherit your assets. You can also set up a trust, which can help you manage your assets during your lifetime and distribute them smoothly after your death while avoiding probate.

Living Will: A living will outlines your healthcare preferences if you become unable to communicate. It specifies the treatments you do or don't want, ensuring that your medical wishes are followed.

Living Trust: Setting up a living trust can be particularly helpful for singles. It allows you to manage your assets during your lifetime, provides instructions for their use if you're incapacitated, and guarantees that they are distributed according to your wishes when you pass away—without going through probate.

Irrevocable Life Insurance Trust (ILIT): This type of trust allows you to remove life insurance proceeds from your taxable estate, ensuring that the payout goes directly to your beneficiaries. For single people with significant assets, this can be an important strategy to minimize estate taxes.

Annual Gifting: If you have considerable assets, gifting is a way to reduce the size of your estate during your lifetime. You can give up to $19,000 (as of 2025) per year, per recipient, tax-free. Over time, this can significantly reduce your taxable estate.

Here are some practical tips for single individuals when setting up an estate plan:

Understand intestate laws. If you don't have a will, state laws will decide who gets your assets, which could be people you wouldn't have chosen. It's crucial to understand these laws and create a plan that overrides them if needed.

Consider a Power of Attorney and healthcare proxy. Appoint someone you trust to make decisions on your behalf if you're incapacitated. A durable power of attorney can handle financial matters, while a healthcare proxy makes medical decisions.

Pay tuition or medical expenses. If you're looking to reduce your estate's size, paying for someone's education or medical expenses directly can be a tax-free way to transfer wealth, and it doesn't count toward the annual gift tax exemption.

Consider gifting assets that are likely to appreciate, such as stock or real estate, before they increase in value. This reduces the future value of your taxable estate and helps lower potential estate taxes.

Identify your heirs. Clearly identify who will inherit your assets. Whether it's family members, friends, or charitable organizations, having this explicitly stated in your will or trust ensures that your wishes are carried out.

Whether through wills, trusts, powers of attorney, or gifting strategies, careful planning will help you avoid legal complications and give you peace of mind that your affairs are in order. It's important to review your estate plan regularly and make updates as your life or financial situation changes.

Taking care of your aging parent or parents is also part of proper estate planning. Respecting the vulnerability of older parents, their rights to privacy, and agency in making their decisions should be considered when you approach them with planning. This particular aspect of caring for aging parents requires sensitivity and careful planning to meet their wishes and to properly manage their assets. As parents age, it's essential to make sure that everything is in order to avoid potential legal and financial complications down the line. Here's a detailed guide on how to approach estate planning for and with aging parents.

As parents grow older, they may become less willing to discuss finances, medical decisions, or future plans. It's important to approach estate planning with patience and understanding. Unlike other estate plans, this process may involve difficult discussions about end-of-life care, healthcare proxies, and ensuring that their financial affairs are handled by someone they trust if they become incapacitated.

Here are key estate planning strategies to ensure that your aging parents' wishes are respected and their assets are protected:

Wills and Trusts: If your parents don't already have a will or trust, help them set one up. A will outlines their wishes for asset distribution, while a trust can help manage assets during their lifetime and avoid probate.

Power of Attorney: Ensure that a durable power of attorney is in place. This document allows a trusted individual to manage your parents' financial affairs if they become unable to do so themselves.

Healthcare Directives: A healthcare proxy or living will ensures that your parents' medical preferences are known and followed if they become incapacitated.

Insurance Policies: Review life insurance policies and long-term care insurance to make sure their coverage is adequate for potential future needs.

Access to Important Documents: It's important to have access to key documents, such as their will, insurance policies, and tax returns, to handle their estate properly when the time comes.

Here are some practical tips to help guide you through estate planning with aging parents:

Set a slower pace for making changes. Understand that this process can be emotionally charged for your parents. Take it step by step, allowing them time to think through their decisions without feeling rushed.

Make a plan to discuss Estate Planning. Approach these conversations carefully. Choose a comfortable setting, and start by explaining why estate planning is important for them and for the family. Make sure they understand that the goal is to honor their wishes.

Identify key people to involve in the process. It's essential to identify who will be involved in managing your parents' affairs. This could include family members or professional advisors like estate attorneys. Everyone involved should be on the same page to avoid conflicts.

Discuss the possibility of an existing will. If your parents already have a will, review it with them to ensure it still reflects their current wishes. If they don't have one, help them get started on creating it.

Talk about Power of Attorney. A durable power of attorney ensures that a trusted person can manage your parents' financial affairs if they're no longer able to. This is a critical part of estate planning for aging parents.

Discuss their end of life wishes. Having a conversation about healthcare directives, such as a living will, ensures that your parents' medical preferences are known and respected. This includes discussing whether they would want life-sustaining treatment in certain situations.

Ask about insurance policies. Review life insurance and long-term care insurance policies to make sure they're up to date and that coverage is sufficient for any potential medical or long-term care needs.

Request access to tax returns and financial documents. Gaining access to financial documents such as tax returns is important for managing their estate and avoiding future complications.

Estate planning with aging parents is a delicate process that requires time, patience, and careful communication. Taking the time to plan with your parents now will provide peace of mind and help avoid unnecessary stress in the future. You will be glad you took these steps once these matters are handled, especially when the time comes to put them into effect.

Married couples have several options to protect their joint and individual assets.

Estate planning for married couples often involves more complex decisions than for single individuals, as both partners typically need to coordinate their assets and ensure that their wishes are aligned. Marriage brings additional legal and financial considerations into estate planning, especially when it comes to taxes, asset distribution, and ensuring both spouses are protected.

When you're married, estate planning decisions impact both you and your spouse. Marriage automatically grants certain legal rights, such as spousal inheritance rights, but without a clear estate plan, things might not go as you intended. Married couples have several benefits in estate planning, such as unlimited marital deduction, which allows spouses to transfer assets to each other tax-free. However, if you don't plan carefully, your assets may not be distributed the way you want between your spouse, (step)children, or other beneficiaries.

Here are some key estate planning strategies and tools for married couples to consider:

Wills and Trusts: Both spouses should have a will in place, clearly stating how their individual and shared assets should be distributed. Trusts can also be beneficial for protecting assets and minimizing taxes.

Bypass Trust (Credit Shelter Trust): This is often used to take advantage of each spouse's estate tax exemption, reducing the overall tax burden on the estate. Upon the death of the first spouse, a portion of the estate goes into a trust for the benefit of the surviving spouse, and the remainder passes tax-free to the heirs.

Durable Power of Attorney and Healthcare Directives: Each spouse should have these in place to ensure that if one becomes incapacitated, the other can make legal, financial, and medical decisions on their behalf.

When planning your estate as a married couple, there are several important factors to keep in mind:

Do you live in a community property state? In community property states, assets acquired during marriage are generally considered jointly owned by both spouses. This can affect how assets are distributed after one spouse passes away. If you live in a community property state, you'll need to be aware of how the law impacts your estate plan.

Should you consider a bypass trust? Bypass trusts (or credit shelter trusts) allow married couples to minimize estate taxes by placing a portion of the estate into a trust for the surviving spouse while still ensuring that the remainder passes to the beneficiaries tax-free. This is especially useful for high-net-worth couples.

What do you want to distribute? Both spouses need to decide what they want to leave behind. This includes assets like real estate, financial accounts, and personal belongings. You should also decide how much each spouse is leaving to each other versus other beneficiaries, such as children or charities.

How will you distribute said assets? Decide how you want your assets to be distributed—whether it's through outright gifts, trusts, or other mechanisms. Trusts can provide more control over how and when assets are distributed, while outright gifts transfer ownership immediately.

How will family dynamics influence the process? Family dynamics can significantly affect estate planning decisions. For example, if either spouse has children from a previous marriage or there are concerns about family conflicts, a carefully structured estate plan can help ensure fairness and prevent disputes.

Is your preferred strategy tax-friendly? Tax efficiency is a crucial consideration in estate planning. Married couples can take advantage of various tax benefits, including marital deduction, which allows for tax-free transfers between spouses. Other strategies, like setting up trusts, can also help minimize estate taxes and protect assets for future generations.

For married couples, estate planning requires coordination and thoughtful decision-making. From considering whether to use trusts to understanding how community property laws affect your estate, it's essential to tailor your plan to meet both spouses' needs and protect your assets. Working together on an estate plan ensures that your wishes are aligned and that your financial future is secure.

Keeping Documents Safe and Accessible

It's important to keep your estate planning documents secure and easy to access. If they're lost or damaged, it can create problems for your loved ones. Storing these documents safely is essential!If your documents—such as will, trust, powers of attorney, healthcare directives, etc.—can't be found or accessed, it can lead to severe and protracted legal headaches for your family. Having these documents in a safe and accessible place is key to avoiding unnecessary issues.

Here's how you can keep your estate planning documents safe while making sure they're accessible:

Make copies of all documents. It's a good idea to have copies of your important documents. You can give these to your executor, close family members, or your attorney. Only share them with trusted individuals to avoid any misuse.

Buy a safe. Get a fireproof and waterproof safe to store your documents at home. This will protect them from fire, water damage, or theft.

Tell your family where the documents are kept. Whether you do purchase a safe or not, it's important that your family or executor knows where to find the documents. Hidden documents are no help if no one can access them when needed.

Talk to your attorney: Your attorney can hold onto your original documents in a secure location, like a law firm vault. Make sure your family knows which attorney has them. Again, this is one of those situations where keeping the estate up-to-date is crucial. If you change attorneys, you need to let your family know that as well. Similarly, if your family circumstances change, you need to inform your attorney.

Use online storage. Consider storing digital copies of your estate documents in a secure online vault. These services allow easy access and often provide encrypted storage. Just make sure your executor or trusted family members have the login info.

Taking steps now to protect your estate planning documents is essential for a successful estate plan. By keeping them safe, sharing their location with trusted people, and using both physical and digital storage options, you're making sure everything is ready when your family needs it the most.

Don't wait to secure your estate plan—start today. Whether it's setting up a will, creating a trust, or simply safeguarding your documents, every action you take now will make a difference later.

Consult with a trusted attorney or financial advisor for personalized guidance. They can help you create a plan that fits your needs.

Congratulations! You have now learned everything you need to know about planning your estate!

Conclusion

By reaching the end of this book, you've taken a major step toward securing your future and protecting your loved ones. Estate planning may not be the most exciting topic, but it's one of the most important things you can do to ensure that your wishes are respected and that your family is taken care of. You've put in the time and the effort to educate yourself, and that deserves recognition. Empowering yourself with proper estate planning will pay off for generations.

But remember, reading this book is only the first step. Now it's time to take action! If you haven't already, start by drafting or reviewing your will, setting up trusts, and making sure your power of attorney and healthcare directives are in place. Using this book as a reference guide, you are fully equipped to secure your future and your assets. Estate planning is a process, and the sooner you start, the more control you'll have over your financial future.

I encourage you to **consult with a trusted estate planning attorney or financial advisor** to help guide you through the specifics of your situation. Each person's estate is unique, and professional guidance will ensure that your plan is tailored to your needs and goals. Don't wait for tomorrow—start today!

This book has been designed to be as practical as possible, giving you concrete templates, tools, and strategies that you can use to start building your estate plan. While these resources can help you make progress, even one small mistake can invalidate your documents. It's always best to have a trusted attorney review your plan to make sure everything is in place correctly. Fortunately, you are equipped to do most of the leg work yourself which will save on legal costs.

Estate planning is an essential part of life, and I challenge you to take action and create or update your plan today. The earlier you start, the more control you'll have over your and your family's financial future. Whether you're protecting your wealth, minimizing taxes, or simply ensuring that your loved ones are taken care of, estate planning puts you in the driver's seat.

Finally, if you found this book helpful, I'd appreciate it if you could leave a review. Your feedback helps others make informed decisions about their own estate planning journey. Thank you for taking the time to read this book—your future and your family's future will be all the better for it. Now – get that plan into action!

Appendices

In the Appendices, you will find valuable resources to help streamline your estate planning process. For your convenience, a downloadable link or QR code is provided, giving you access to the following essential documents:

- Estate Planning Worksheet
- Net Worth Worksheet
- Beneficiary Designations Form
- Will Toolkit
- Trust Toolkit
- Incapacity Planning Toolkit
- Probate Laws by State

These tools have been designed to simplify the process of organizing and managing your estate planning. Simply follow the link or scan the QR code to download and customize these forms for your personal use before you approach an attorney for their legal advice.

https://annaeiken.com/estate-planning-toolkit

Open the Doors to Estate Planning for Everyone

Now that you've reached the end of this book, you're equipped with the tools and knowledge to make informed decisions about wills, trusts, and tax strategies that align with your goals. I hope this journey has shown you that estate planning doesn't have to be daunting—taking the time to make a few important choices today can save your loved ones from unnecessary stress tomorrow.

Your experience and insights could be the key to breaking someone else's cycle of worry. By sharing your review, you can show others just how manageable and empowering estate planning can be.

IN UNDER 1 MINUTE
YOU CAN HELP OTHERS JUST LIKE YOU BY LEAVING A REVIEW!

Thank you for your support. Your words have the potential to inspire others and help them secure a brighter future for themselves and their families.

Scan the QR code to leave your review on Amazon.

Bibliography

SmartAsset. (n.d.). All about the estate tax. Retrieved from https://smartasset.com/taxes/all-about-the-estate-tax

Koley Jessen. (2024). Increased gift and estate tax. Retrieved from https://www.koleyjessen.com/insights/publications/increased-gift-and-estate-tax-2024

Trust & Will. (2024). 2024 tax exemption amounts. Retrieved from https://trustandwill.com/learn/2024-tax-exemption-amounts

SmartAsset. (n.d.). All about the estate tax. Retrieved from https://smartasset.com/taxes/all-about-the-estate-tax

AARP. (2020). States with estate and inheritance taxes. Retrieved from https://www.aarp.org/money/taxes/info-2020/states-with-estate-inheritance-taxes.html

Everplans. (n.d.). State-by-state estate and inheritance tax rates. Retrieved from https://www.everplans.com/articles/state-by-state-estate-and-inheritance-tax-rates

Kiplinger. (n.d.). States with scary death taxes. Retrieved from https://www.kiplinger.com/retirement/inheritance/601551/states-with-scary-death-taxes

Rhode Island Department of Taxation. (2024). Form 706. Retrieved from https://tax.ri.gov/sites/g/files/xkgbur541/files/2024-02/RI-706_w.pdf

IRS. (n.d.). Instructions for Form 706. Retrieved from https://www.irs.gov/pub/irs-pdf/i706.pdf

Denton Estate Planning Lawyer. (n.d.). 12 inspirational quotes about estate planning. Retrieved from https://dentonestateplanninglawyer.com/12-inspirational-quotes-about-estate-planning/

Investopedia. (n.d.). Estate planning. Retrieved from https://www.investopedia.com/terms/e/estateplanning.asp

Nelson Law Group. (n.d.). 10 inspirational quotes about estate planning. Retrieved from https://nelsonlawgrouppc.com/10-inspirational-quotes-about-estate-planning/

Coastal Wealth Management. (n.d.). Famous people who died without proper planning. Retrieved from https://www.coastalwealthmanagement24.com/famous-people-who-died-without-proper-planning/

Estate Law Atlanta. (n.d.). The importance of estate planning: Lessons from celebrities who died without a plan. Retrieved from https://estatelawatlanta.com/the-importance-of-estate-planning-lessons-from-celebrities-who-died-without-a-plan/

Coastal Wealth Management. (2023). Lifestyles of the rich and famous: A Hollywood saga on celebrity estate planning disasters. Retrieved from https://www.crlaw.com/wp-content/uploads/2023/01/Lifestyles-of-the-Rich-and-Famous-A-Hollywood-Saga-on-Celebrity-Estate-Planning-Disasters.pdf

Investopedia. (n.d.). Estate planning. Retrieved from https://www.investopedia.com/terms/e/estateplanning.asp

Trust & Will. (n.d.). What is estate planning? Retrieved from https://trustandwill.com/learn/what-is-estate-planning

Nationwide. (n.d.). What is estate planning? Retrieved from https://www.nationwide.com/lc/resources/investing-and-retirement/articles/what-is-estate-planning

EstatePlanning.com. (n.d.). What is estate planning? Retrieved from https://www.estateplanning.com/what-is-estate-planning

Investopedia. (2015). 4 reasons estate planning is so important. Retrieved from https://www.investopedia.com/articles/wealth-management/122915/4-reasons-estate-planning-so-important.asp

Manulife. (n.d.). 5 reasons why estate planning is important. Retrieved from https://www.manulife.com.ph/about-us/blog/5-reasons-why-estate-planning-is-important.html

Investopedia. (2007). Estate plan checklist. Retrieved from https://www.investopedia.com/articles/pf/07/estate_plan_checklist.asp#toc-2-durable-power-of-attorney

Nationwide. (n.d.). What is estate planning? Retrieved from https://www.nationwide.com/lc/resources/investing-and-retirement/articles/what-is-estate-planning

Davis Toft Law. (n.d.). What are 5 components of estate planning? Retrieved from https://www.davistoftlaw.com/what-are-5-components-estate-planning/

Trust & Will. (n.d.). Estate planning misconceptions. Retrieved from https://trustandwill.com/learn/estate-planning-misconceptions

Walker, T. (n.d.). Common myths about estate planning. Retrieved from https://www.traviswalkerlaw.com/blog/common-myths-about-estate-planning/

Margerie Law. (n.d.). Estate planning misconceptions. Retrieved from https://www.margerielaw.com/estate-planning-misconceptions/

Michigan Law Center. (n.d.). Benefits of early planning. Retrieved from https://www.michiganlawcenter.com/blog/benefits-of-early-planning

Jennings Law. (n.d.). Benefits of early estate planning. Retrieved from https://ljenningslaw.com/benefits-of-early-estate-planning/

Norton Basu. (2021, March). The importance of early estate planning. Retrieved from https://www.nortonbasu.com/blog/2021/03/the-importance-of-early-estate-planning/

DiRon Rutty LLC. (n.d.). Reasons to start estate planning early. Retrieved from https://www.dironruttyllc.com/reasons-to-start-estate-planning-early/

The Business Quotes. (n.d.). Robert Kiyosaki quotes. Retrieved from https://www.thebusinessquotes.com/robert-kiyosaki-quotes/

Northstar Financial. (n.d.). Net worth. Retrieved from https://www.northstarfinancial.com/news-events/net-worth/

Investopedia. (n.d.). Asset. Retrieved from https://www.investopedia.com/terms/a/asset.asp

Indeed. (n.d.). Types of assets. Retrieved from https://www.indeed.com/career-advice/career-development/types-of-assets

Coastal Advice Group. (n.d.). 5 steps on how to be effective in your estate planning. Retrieved from https://coastaladvicegroup.com.au/blog/5-steps-on-how-to-be-effective-in-your-estate-planning/

ASG Investigations. (n.d.). Importance of asset searches in estate planning. Retrieved from https://asginvestigations.com/attorney-services/importance-of-asset-searches-in-estate-planning/

Investopedia. (n.d.). Estate planning checklist. Retrieved from https://www.investopedia.com/articles/retirement/10/estate-planning-checklist.asp

WikiHow. (n.d.). Make a list of personal assets. Retrieved from https://www.wikihow.com/Make-a-List-of-Personal-Assets

LawDepot. (n.d.). Personal asset inventory. Retrieved from https://www.lawdepot.com/resources/estate-articles/personal-asset-inventory/

Oboloo. (n.d.). Why asset valuation matters: Understanding the value of your business. Retrieved from https://oboloo.com/why-asset-valuation-matters-understanding-the-value-of-your-business

Corporate Finance Institute. (n.d.). Asset valuation. Retrieved from https://corporatefinanceinstitute.com/resources/valuation/asset-valuation/

Investopedia. (n.d.). Asset valuation. Retrieved from https://www.investopedia.com/terms/a/assetvaluation.asp

Investopedia. (n.d.). Liability. Retrieved from https://www.investopedia.com/terms/l/liability.asp

The Forage. (n.d.). Liabilities. Retrieved from https://www.theforage.com/blog/skills/liabilities

Marine Credit Union. (n.d.). Estate planning: Assets and liabilities. Retrieved from https://www.marinecu.com/estate-planning-assets-and-liabilities/

Patriot Software. (n.d.). Assets vs. liabilities. Retrieved from https://www.patriotsoftware.com/blog/accounting/assets-vs-liabilities/

Ricaforte Law. (n.d.). Itemizing your debts as part of your estate plan in New York. Retrieved from https://www.ricafortelaw.com/blog/itemizing-your-debts-as-part-of-your-estate-plan-in-new-york.cfm

JGC Group. (n.d.). How to handle your estate planning when a large amount of debt is involved. Retrieved from https://jgcg.com/how-to-handle-your-estate-planning-when-a-large-amount-of-debt-is-involved/

Charles Schwab. (n.d.). Asset inventory worksheet. Retrieved from https://www.schwab.com/resource/asset-inventory-worksheet

Charles Schwab. (n.d.). Net worth worksheet. Retrieved from https://www.schwab.com/public/file/P-6976466/Net-Worth-Worksheet.pdf

Salk Institute for Biological Studies. (n.d.). Be a good ancestor. Retrieved from https://www.salk.edu/be-a-good-ancestor/

Investopedia. (n.d.). Beneficiary. Retrieved from https://www.investopedia.com/terms/b/beneficiary.asp

Bank of America. (n.d.). Estate beneficiaries. Retrieved from https://www.private bank.bankofamerica.com/financial-education/estate-beneficiaries.html

Plannera. (n.d.). Beneficiary designation. Retrieved from https://pepp.plannera.ca/insights/beneficiary-designation

Ameriprise Financial. (n.d.). Designation of beneficiary. Retrieved from https://www.ameriprise.com/financial-goals-priorities/family-estate/designation-of-beneficiary

Creative Planning. (n.d.). Considerations when choosing beneficiaries. Retrieved from https://creativeplanning.com/insights/estate-planning/considerations-choosing-beneficiaries/

AWMLaw. (2023, September). How should you choose your beneficiaries? Retrieved from https://www.awmlaw.com/blog/2023/09/how-should-you-choose-your-beneficiaries/

Will Protect. (n.d.). Beneficiary choices. Retrieved from https://willprotect.co.uk/beneficiary-choices/

FreeWill. (n.d.). Per stirpes vs. per capita. Retrieved from https://www.freewill.com/learn/per-stirpes-vs-per-capita

Investopedia. (n.d.). Per stirpes. Retrieved from https://www.investopedia.com/terms/p/perstirpes.asp

FindLaw. (n.d.). Per stirpes and per capita distribution under a will. Retrieved from https://www.findlaw.com/forms/resources/estate-planning/last-will-and-testament/per-stirpes-and-per-capita-distribution-under-a-will-what-does-it-mean.html

Wells Fargo Advisors. (n.d.). Beneficiary designation tips. Retrieved from https://www.wellsfargoadvisors.com/planning/goals/estate-planning/beneficiary-designation-tips.htm

Hunter Benefits. (n.d.). Beneficiary designation forms: A guide to avoiding legal pitfalls. Retrieved from https://hunterbenefits.com/beneficiary-designation-forms-a-guide-to-avoiding-legal-pitfalls/

U.S. Office of Personnel Management. (n.d.). Standard Form 1152: Beneficiary designation form. Retrieved from https://www.opm.gov/forms/pdf_fill/sf-1152.pdf

Grand Valley State University. (n.d.). Beneficiary designation form (Michigan). Retrieved from https://www.gvsu.edu/cms4/asset/614589D9-D87D-F688-4E9414B96B94C137/beneficiary_designation_form_mi.pdf

Wisconsin Department of Employee Trust Funds. (n.d.). How to fill out beneficiary designation (Alternate ET-2321). Retrieved from https://etf.wi.gov/resource/how-fill-out-beneficiary-designation-alternate-et-2321

Ferris State University. (n.d.). Instructions to complete beneficiary designation. Retrieved from https://www.ferris.edu/administration/adminandfinance/human/Benefits/pdfs-docs/Beneficiary_Info/MESSA_Instrcutions_to_complete_Beneficiary_Designation.pdf

Grand Valley State University. (n.d.). Beneficiary designation form (Michigan). Retrieved from https://www.gvsu.edu/cms4/asset/614589D9-D87D-F688-4E9414B96B94C137/beneficiary_designation_form_mi.pdf

Society for Human Resource Management (SHRM). (n.d.). Beneficiary designation form. Retrieved from https://www.shrm.org/topics-tools/tools/forms/beneficiary-designation-form

Quotes.net. (n.d.). Vince Lombardi quote. Retrieved from https://www.quotes.net/quote/5571

Investopedia. (n.d.). What is a will? Retrieved from https://www.investopedia.com/articles/pf/08/what-is-a-will.asp

CDC Foundation. (n.d.). Will. Retrieved from https://www.cdcfoundation.org/give/will

American Bar Association. (n.d.). Introduction to wills. Retrieved from https://www.americanbar.org/groups/real_property_trust_estate/resources/estate-planning/intro-wills/

Government of New South Wales. (n.d.). Learn about wills. Retrieved from https://www.nsw.gov.au/family-and-relationships/planning-for-end-of-life/learn-about-wills

LegalZoom. (n.d.). What are the 4 types of wills and what should they include? Retrieved from https://www.legalzoom.com/articles/what-are-the-4-types-of-wills-and-what-should-they-include

MetLife. (n.d.). Types of wills. Retrieved from https://www.metlife.com/stories/legal/types-of-wills/

Forbes. (n.d.). Types of wills. Retrieved from https://www.forbes.com/advisor/legal/estate-law/types-wills/

Palm City Lawyer. (n.d.). Important elements of a will. Retrieved from https://palmcitylawyer.com/blog/important-elements-of-a-will/

FindLaw. (n.d.). What is a valid will? Retrieved from https://www.findlaw.-

com/forms/resources/estate-planning/last-will-and-testament/what-is-a-valid-will.html

Personal Finance Extension. (n.d.). Elements of a valid will. Retrieved from https://personal-finance.extension.org/elements-of-a-valid-will/

Graham Thompson. (2020, March). General will template. Retrieved from https://grahamthompson.com/wp-content/uploads/2020/03/GENERAL-WILL-TEMPLATE.pdf

LawShelf. (n.d.). Wills and provisions (module 1 of 5). Retrieved from https://www.lawshelf.com/videocoursesmoduleview/wills-and-provisions-module-1-of-5

BMC Estate Planning. (n.d.). Provisions in your last will and testament. Retrieved from https://www.bmcestateplanning.com/blog/provisions-in-your-last-will-testament

The Probate Guy. (n.d.). Four common will provisions and the reasons behind them. Retrieved from https://www.theprobateguy.com/four-common-will-provisions-and-the-reasons-behind-them/

LawShelf. (n.d.). Last wills and testaments: Common provisions and their purposes. Retrieved from https://www.lawshelf.com/shortvideoscontentview/last-wills-and-testaments-common-will-provisions-and-their-purpsoses

Estate and Probate Lawyer. (n.d.). Three common will provisions and their rationales. Retrieved from https://estateandprobatelawyer.com/3-common-will-provisions-and-the-rationales-behind-them/

LegalZoom. (n.d.). State requirements for a last will. Retrieved from https://www.legalzoom.com/articles/state-requirements-for-a-last-will

FreeWill. (n.d.). How to make a will. Retrieved from https://www.freewill.com/learn/how-to-make-a-will

Forbes. (n.d.). How to write a will. Retrieved from https://www.forbes.com/advisor/legal/estate-law/how-to-write-a-will/

LegalZoom. (n.d.). How to write a will. Retrieved from https://www.legalzoom.com/articles/how-to-write-a-will

Get Amiri Legal. (n.d.). Sample will. Retrieved from https://www.getamirilegal.com/articles/sample-will

BrainyQuote. (n.d.). Vince Lombardi quote. Retrieved from https://www.brainyquote.com/quotes/vince_lombardi_382625

Investopedia. (n.d.). Living trust. Retrieved from https://www.investopedia.com/terms/l/living-trust.asp

EstatePlanning.com. (n.d.). Understanding living trusts. Retrieved from https://www.estateplanning.com/understanding-living-trusts

FreeWill. (n.d.). What is a living trust? Retrieved from https://www.freewill.-

com/learn/what-is-a-living-trust

Racine Law. (n.d.). The four main reasons people use trusts in their estate planning. Retrieved from https://www.racinelaw.net/the-four-main-reasons-people-use-trusts-in-their-estate-planning.html

U.S. Bank. (n.d.). Benefits of setting up a trust. Retrieved from https://www.usbank.com/wealth-management/financial-perspectives/trust-and-estate-planning/benefits-of-setting-up-a-trust.html

Iowa State University Extension and Outreach. (n.d.). Whole farm. Retrieved from https://www.extension.iastate.edu/agdm/wholefarm/html/c4-59.html

Forbes. (n.d.). Living trust vs. will: Differences, pros & cons. Retrieved from https://www.forbes.com/advisor/legal/estate-law/living-trust-vs-will/

FreeWill. (n.d.). How to set up a trust fund. Retrieved from https://www.freewill.com/learn/how-to-set-up-a-trust-fund/

Bank of America. (n.d.). Understanding trusts. Retrieved from https://www.privatebank.bankofamerica.com/financial-education/understanding-trusts.html

Investopedia. (n.d.). Trust fund. Retrieved from https://www.investopedia.com/terms/t/trust-fund.asp#toc-revocable-trust-funds-vs-irrevocable-trust-funds

Investopedia. (n.d.). What is the difference between revocable trust and living trust? Retrieved from https://www.investopedia.com/ask/answers/071615/what-difference-between-revocable-trust-and-living-trust.asp

Western & Southern Financial Group. (n.d.). What are the different types of trusts? Retrieved from https://www.westernsouthern.com/retirement/what-are-the-different-types-of-trusts

FindLaw. (n.d.). Types of trusts. Retrieved from https://www.findlaw.com/estate/trusts/types-of-trusts.html

Investopedia. (n.d.). Trust basics. Retrieved from https://www.investopedia.com/articles/pf/08/trust-basics.asp#toc-common-types-of-trusts

PolicyGenius. (n.d.). How to distribute trust assets to beneficiaries. Retrieved from https://www.policygenius.com/trusts/how-to-distribute-trust-assets-to-beneficiaries/

Trust & Will. (n.d.). Trust fund distribution to beneficiaries. Retrieved from https://trustandwill.com/learn/trust-fund-distribution-to-beneficiaries

Moghullaw. (2024, March). Key asset protection clauses to include in a trust agreement. Retrieved from https://moghullaw.com/2024/03/key-asset-protection-clauses-to-include-in-a-trust-agreement/

Jones, L. (n.d.). Standard clauses to include in your trust. Retrieved from https://www.linkedin.com/pulse/standard-clauses-include-your-trust-lauren-jones/

Monk Legal. (2021, November 27). Clauses to include in your revocable trust.

Retrieved from https://monklegal.com/lawyer/2021/11/27/Estate-Planning/Clauses-to-Include-in-Your-Revocable-Trust_bl42582.htm

JGCG. (n.d.). Clauses to include in your revocable trust. Retrieved from https://jgcg.com/clauses-to-include-in-your-revocable-trust/

FreeWill. (n.d.). How to set up a trust fund. Retrieved from https://www.freewill.com/learn/how-to-set-up-a-trust-fund/

Forbes. (n.d.). How to set up a trust. Retrieved from https://www.forbes.com/advisor/legal/estate-law/how-set-up-trust/

Investopedia. (n.d.). How to set up a trust fund. Retrieved fromhttps://www.investopedia.com/articles/pf/12/set-up-a-trust-fund.asp

Basel Governance. (2021, June). Example trust deed. Retrieved from https://baselgovernance.org/sites/default/files/2021-06/Example%20Trust%20Deed%20final%2024.6.21.pdf

AdvocateKhoj. (n.d.). Trust agreements. Retrieved fromhttps://www.advocatekhoj.com/library/agreements/trust/6.php

Sloan DeLaney, K. (2016, Spring). Sample of a revocable trust. Retrieved fromhttps://nysba.org/NYSBA/Coursebooks/Spring%202016%20CLE%20Coursebooks/Spring%202016%20Estate%20Planning%20and%20Will%20Drafting/4KarinSloanDeLaneySampleofaRevocableTrust.pdf

Positum. (n.d.). Anatomy of trust. Retrieved from https://www.positum.org/anatomy-of-trust-ignatova/

Blacksburg Law. (n.d.). The role of a power of attorney in estate planning. Retrieved from https://blacksburg-law.com/insights/the-role-of-a-power-of-attorney-in-estate-planning/

Investopedia. (n.d.). Power of attorney. Retrieved from https://www.investopedia.com/terms/p/powerofattorney.asp

SeniorLiving.org. (n.d.). Power of attorney: Differences and importance. Retrieved from https://www.seniorliving.org/finance/estate-planning/power-attorney/#difference

FreeWill. (n.d.). How to make a power of attorney. Retrieved from https://www.freewill.com/learn/how-to-make-a-power-of-attorney

MetLife. (n.d.). How to get power of attorney. Retrieved from https://www.metlife.com/stories/legal/how-to-get-power-of-attorney/

MSD Manuals. (n.d.). Health care power of attorney. Retrieved from https://www.msdmanuals.com/home/fundamentals/legal-and-ethical-issues/advance-directives#Health-Care-Power-of-Attorney_v715014

Johns Hopkins Medicine. (n.d.). Advance directives. Retrieved from https://www.hopkinsmedicine.org/patient-care/patients-visitors/advance-directives

National Institute on Aging. (n.d.). Preparing a living will. Retrieved from https://www.nia.nih.gov/health/advance-care-planning/preparing-living-will

LifePlan Legal. (n.d.). Medical power of attorney vs durable power of attorney: Understanding the differences. Retrieved from https://lifeplanlegalaz.com/medical-power-of-attorney-vs-durable-power-of-attorney-understanding-the-differences/

eForms. (n.d.). Durable vs medical power of attorney and why you need both. Retrieved from https://learn.eforms.com/estate-planning/durable-vs-medical-power-of-attorney-and-why-you-need-both/

Forbes. (n.d.). How to make a living will. Retrieved from https://www.forbes.com/advisor/legal/estate-law/how-make-living-will/

Legal Templates. (n.d.). Living will form. Retrieved from https://legaltemplates.net/form/living-will/

JotForm. (n.d.). Medical power of attorney form. Retrieved from https://www.jotform.com/pdf-templates/medical-power-of-attorney-form

Legal Templates. (n.d.). Living will. Retrieved from https://legaltemplates.net/form/living-will/

JotForm. (n.d.). Durable power of attorney form. Retrieved from https://www.jotform.com/form-templates/durable-power-of-attorney-form

Queens Probate Lawyer. (n.d.). Probate by the numbers. Retrieved from https://www.queens-probatelawyer.com/probate-by-the-numbers/

Investopedia. (n.d.). Probate. Retrieved from https://www.investopedia.com/terms/p/probate.asp

Forbes. (n.d.). What is probate? Retrieved from https://www.forbes.com/advisor/legal/estate-law/what-is-probate/

FindLaw. (n.d.). Probate process without a will. Retrieved from https://www.findlaw.com/estate/probate/probate-process-without-a-will.html

Gayheart & Willis. (n.d.). Factors that affect the length of probate. Retrieved from https://www.gayheartandwillis.com/the-factors-that-can-affect-the-length-of-probate

Everplans. (n.d.). State-by-state probate laws. Retrieved from https://www.everplans.com/articles/state-by-state-probate-laws

FindLaw. (n.d.). State laws on estates and probate. Retrieved from https://www.findlaw.com/estate/planning-an-estate/state-laws-estates-probate.html

Doane & Doane. (n.d.). 5 proven probate avoidance strategies for estate planning. Retrieved from https://www.doaneanddoane.com/5-proven-probate-avoidance-strategies-for-estate-planning

Easler Law. (n.d.). What are common probate avoidance strategies? Retrieved from https://easlerlaw.com/faq/what-are-common-probate-avoidance-strategies

Cavitch. (2024, April). Benefits and strategies to avoid probate. Retrieved from https://www.cavitch.com/blog/2024/04/benefits-and-strategies-to-avoid-probate/

Tli7f, K. (n.d.). Avoiding probate: 4 simple strategies. Retrieved from https://www.linkedin.com/pulse/avoiding-probate-4-simple-strategies-estate-planning-kiuma-tli7f/

Forbes. (n.d.). Estate taxes. Retrieved from https://www.forbes.com/advisor/taxes/estate-taxes/

Investopedia. (n.d.). Estate tax. Retrieved from https://www.investopedia.com/terms/e/estatetax.asp

Investopedia. (n.d.). Estate taxes: Who pays what and how much. Retrieved from https://www.investopedia.com/articles/personal-finance/120715/estate-taxes-who-pays-what-and-how-much.asp

CNBC. (n.d.). What is estate tax and who pays it? Retrieved from https://www.cnbc.com/select/what-is-estate-tax-and-who-pays-it/

SmartAsset. (n.d.). All about the estate tax. Retrieved from https://smartasset.com/taxes/all-about-the-estate-tax

Anderson Advisors. (n.d.). Estate tax exemption: How much it is and how to calculate it. Retrieved from https://andersonadvisors.com/estate-tax-exemption-how-much-it-is-and-how-to-calculate-it/

FindLaw. (n.d.). 10 ways to reduce estate taxes. Retrieved from https://www.findlaw.com/estate/planning-an-estate/10-ways-to-reduce-estate-taxes.html

Fidelity. (n.d.). How to avoid estate taxes. Retrieved from https://www.fidelity.com/learning-center/personal-finance/how-to-avoid-estate-taxes

Investopedia. (n.d.). 7 reasons to own life insurance in an irrevocable trust. Retrieved from https://www.investopedia.com/articles/personal-finance/092315/7-reasons-own-life-insurance-irrevocable-trust.asp

Investopedia. (n.d.). Irrevocable life insurance trust (ILIT). Retrieved from https://www.investopedia.com/ask/answers/10/irrevocable-life-insurance-trust.asp

Northwestern Mutual. (n.d.). What is an irrevocable life insurance trust? Retrieved from https://www.northwesternmutual.com/life-and-money/what-is-an-irrevocable-life-insurance-trust/

FreshBooks. (n.d.). Unified tax credit. Retrieved from https://www.freshbooks.com/glossary/tax/unified-tax-credit?srsltid=AfmBOooBjkzY-ky70_wttxGvAs-D8ScsM-dFC_g3rJTqLJOz7EBuS_GTV

SmartAsset. (n.d.). Unified credit. Retrieved from https://smartasset.com/taxes/unified-credit

Investopedia. (n.d.). Unified tax credit. Retrieved from https://www.investopedia.com/terms/u/unified-tax-credit.asp

Investopedia. (n.d.). Estate tax exemption 2021. Retrieved from https://www.investopedia.com/estate-tax-exemption-2021-definition-5114715

AARP. (n.d.). States with estate and inheritance taxes. Retrieved from https://www.aarp.org/money/taxes/info-2020/states-with-estate-inheritance-taxes.html

Tax Foundation. (n.d.). State estate and inheritance taxes 2023. Retrieved from https://taxfoundation.org/data/all/state/state-estate-tax-inheritance-tax-2023/

American College of Trust and Estate Counsel (ACTEC). (n.d.). Estate tax returns. Retrieved from https://www.actec.org/resource-center/video/estate-tax-returns/

Investopedia. (n.d.). Form 706: Estate tax return. Retrieved from https://www.investopedia.com/terms/f/form-706.asp

Rhode Island Division of Taxation. (n.d.). RI-706 form. Retrieved from https://tax.ri.gov/sites/g/files/xkgbur541/files/2024-02/RI-706_w.pdf

Internal Revenue Service (IRS). (n.d.). Instructions for Form 706. Retrieved from https://www.irs.gov/pub/irs-pdf/i706.pdf

Rhode Island Division of Taxation. (n.d.). RI-706 form (duplicate). Retrieved from https://tax.ri.gov/sites/g/files/xkgbur541/files/2024-02/RI-706_w.pdf

Finance Strategists. (n.d.). Estate planning costs. Retrieved from https://www.financestrategists.com/estate-planning-lawyer/estate-planning-cost/

Doane & Doane. (n.d.). How much does estate planning cost? A comprehensive guide. Retrieved from https://www.doaneanddoane.com/how-much-does-estate-planning-cost-a-comprehensive-guide

Rilus Law. (n.d.). What is the average estate planning cost? Retrieved from https://www.riluslaw.com/blog/what-is-the-average-estate-planning-cost

SmartAsset. (n.d.). Estate planning costs. Retrieved from https://smartasset.com/estate-planning/estate-planning-costs

Investopedia. (n.d.). 10 questions to ask your estate planning attorney. Retrieved from https://www.investopedia.com/articles/personal-finance/070815/10-questions-ask-your-estate-planning-attorney.asp

Geiger Law Office. (n.d.). 11 tips for choosing the right estate planning attorney for you. Retrieved from https://www.geigerlawoffice.com/library/11-tips-for-choosing-the-right-estate-planning-attorney-for-you.cfm

Rhodes Law Firm PC. (n.d.). How to choose an estate planning attorney. Retrieved from https://www.rhodeslawfirmpc.com/how-to-choose-an-estate-planning-law-attorney/

FindLaw. (n.d.). Estate planning mistakes. Retrieved from https://www.findlaw.com/forms/resources/estate-planning/estate-planning-mistakes.html

Fidelity. (n.d.). Estate planning common pitfalls. Retrieved from https://www.fidelity.com/viewpoints/wealth-management/estate-planning-common-pitfalls

Z Family Law. (n.d.). Estate planning pitfalls. Retrieved from https://www.zfamilylaw.com/blog/estate-planning-pitfalls

Sprouse Law Firm. (n.d.). Estate planning attorneys vs. DIY estate planning services. Retrieved from https://www.sprouselaw.com/estate-planning-attorneys-vs-diy-estate-planning-services/

Pile Law. (n.d.). DIY estate planning pitfalls: The risks of creating your own documents in Pennsylvania. Retrieved from https://pilelaw.com/diy-estate-planning-pitfalls-the-risks-of-creating-your-own-documents-in-pennsylvania/

Bogutz & Gordon. (2024, March). Beware the dangers of DIY estate planning. Retrieved from https://www.bogutzandgordon.com/blog/2024/03/beware-the-dangers-of-diy-estate-planning/

LinkedIn. (n.d.). Navigating estate planning costs: Texas strategies. Retrieved from https://www.linkedin.com/pulse/navigating-estate-planning-costs-texas-strategies-uxotf/

Tuller Law. (2019, January 3). 3 ways to minimize estate planning fees. Retrieved from https://www.tullerlaw.com/blog1/2019/1/3/3-ways-to-minimize-estate-planning-fees

Caitlyn Ashley Law. (n.d.). 10 motivational quotes about estate planning. Retrieved from https://www.caitlynashleylaw.com/post/10-motivational-quotes-about-estate-planning

Personal Family Lawyer. (n.d.). 5 reasons why you need to review your estate plan. Retrieved from https://personalfamilylawyer.com/articles/5-reasons-why-you-need-to-review-your-estate-plan

Legal Sweeney. (n.d.). How often should you review your estate plan? Retrieved from https://www.legalsweeney.com/how-often-should-you-review-your-estate-plan/

Fidelity. (n.d.). Reviewing and updating your estate plan. Retrieved from https://www.fidelity.com/life-events/estate-planning/update-estate-plan

Fidelity. (n.d.). Update estate plan: Reviewing your plan at regular intervals. Retrieved from https://www.fidelity.com/life-events/estate-planning/update-estate-plan

Wiggin and Dana LLP. (n.d.). 10 reasons to update your estate plan. Retrieved from https://www.wiggin.com/publication/10-reasons-to-update-your-estate-plan/

Origin. (n.d.). Things to consider when updating your estate plan. Retrieved from https://www.useorigin.com/resources/blog/things-to-consider-when-updating-your-estate-plan

Lawyer Monthly. (2022, December). What happens if you don't update your estate plan? Retrieved from https://www.lawyer-monthly.com/2022/12/what-happens-if-you-dont-update-your-estate-plan/

Whipple Law Group. (n.d.). Updating your estate plans. Retrieved from https://www.whiplawgroup.com/updating-your-estate-plans/

Crue. (n.d.). Stepping into your shoes: The important role of your executor. Retrieved from https://crue.co.za/stepping-into-your-shoes-the-important-role-of-your-executor/

Investopedia. (n.d.). Executor. Retrieved from https://www.investopedia.com/terms/e/executor.asp

CoverMe. (n.d.). How to choose the right executor for your will. Retrieved from https://www.coverme.com/blog/life/how-to-choose-right-executor-for-your-will.html?province=ON&agecode=0

Investopedia. (n.d.). Trustee. Retrieved from https://www.investopedia.com/terms/t/trustee.asp

EstatePlanning.com. (n.d.). Duties and responsibilities of a trustee. Retrieved from https://www.estateplanning.com/duties-and-responsibilities-of-a-trustee

Forbes. (2019, May 31). How to choose a trustee. Retrieved from https://www.forbes.com/sites/christinefletcher/2019/05/31/how-to-choose-a-trustee/

U.S. Bank. (n.d.). How to choose a trustee of a trust. Retrieved from https://www.usbank.com/wealth-management/financial-perspectives/trust-and-estate-planning/how-to-choose-a-trustee-of-a-trust.html

Creative Planning. (n.d.). Estate planning for blended families. Retrieved from https://creativeplanning.com/insights/estate-planning/estate-planning-blended-families/

Trust & Will. (n.d.). Estate planning for blended families. Retrieved from https://trustandwill.com/learn/estate-planning-for-blended-families

RBC Wealth Management. (n.d.). Estate planning for blended families: Four tips on getting it right. Retrieved from https://www.rbcwealthmanagement.com/en-ca/insights/estate-planning-for-blended-families-4-tips-on-getting-it-right

Fidelity. (n.d.). Estate planning for singles. Retrieved from https://www.fidelity.com/viewpoints/wealth-management/estate-planning-for-singles

AARP. (2023). Estate planning for singles. Retrieved from https://www.aarp.org/money/investing/info-2023/estate-planning-for-singles.html

Porte Brown. (n.d.). Estate tax planning tips for single people. Retrieved from https://www.portebrown.com/newsblog-archive/estate-tax-planning-tips-for-single-people

LegalZoom. (n.d.). Estate planning for the single person. Retrieved from https://www.legalzoom.com/articles/estate-planning-for-the-single-person

Kiplinger. (n.d.). Estate planning for aging parents: A delicate balance. Retrieved from https://www.kiplinger.com/retirement/estate-planning-for-aging-parents-a-delicate-balance

Elville Associates. (n.d.). Eight tips for having the talk about estate planning with elderly parents. Retrieved from https://elvilleassociates.com/eight-tips-for-having-the-talk-about-estate-planning-with-elderly-parents/

LifePlan Legal AZ. (n.d.). Estate planning strategies to care for aging parents.

Retrieved from https://lifeplanlegalaz.com/estate-planning-strategies-to-care-for-aging-parents/

American Century. (n.d.). Estate planning for elderly parents: How to. Retrieved from https://www.americancentury.com/insights/estate-planning-for-elderly-parents-how-to/

LawDepot. (n.d.). Estate planning for married couples. Retrieved from https://www.lawdepot.com/resources/estate-articles/estate-planning-for-married-couples/?loc=US

Trust & Will. (n.d.). Estate planning for married couples. Retrieved from https://trustandwill.com/learn/estate-planning-for-married-couples

ARAG Legal. (n.d.). Estate planning for married couples. Retrieved from https://www.araglegal.com/individuals/learning-center/topics/family-and-relationships/estate-planning-for-married-couples

Rocket Lawyer. (n.d.). Estate planning for married couples. Retrieved from https://www.rocketlawyer.com/family-and-personal/estate-planning/estate-planning-preparation/legal-guide/focus-on-financial-planning-estate-planning-for-married-couples

Redwood Financial. (n.d.). Safeguarding your legacy: The importance of secure estate planning storage. Retrieved from https://redwoodfinancial.co.uk/safeguarding-your-legacy-the-importance-of-secure-estate-planning-storage/

BMC Estate Planning. (n.d.). Keeping your estate planning documents safe. Retrieved from https://www.bmcestateplanning.com/blog/keeping-your-estate-planning-documents-safe

FindLaw. (n.d.). How to keep your estate planning documents safe. Retrieved from https://www.findlaw.com/forms/resources/estate-planning/how-to-keep-your-estate-planning-documents-safe.html

SmartAsset. (n.d.). *All about the estate tax*. SmartAsset. https://smartasset.com/taxes/all-about-the-estate-tax

Made in the USA
Monee, IL
12 November 2024